Every Woman Is a World

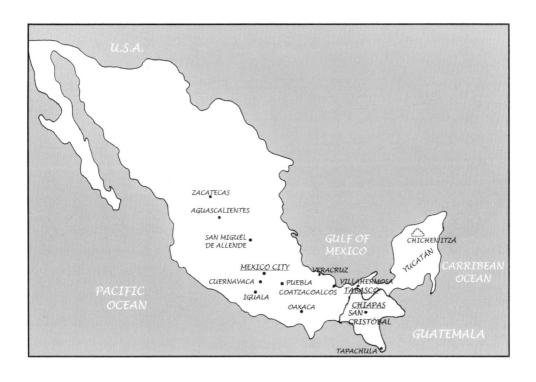

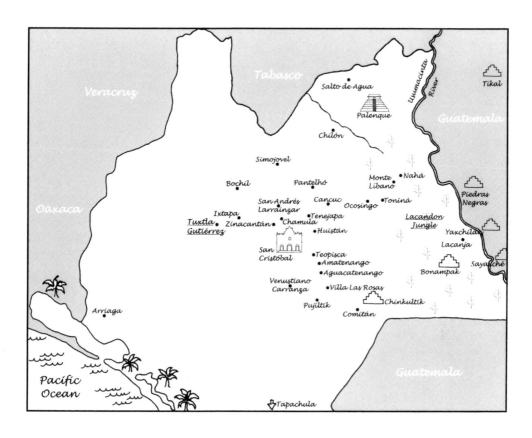

BOOK EIGHTEEN

Louann Atkins Temple Women & Culture Series

Every Woman Is a World

Interviews with Women of Chiapas

Gayle Walker and Kiki Suárez

Edited by Carol Karasik
Foreword by Elena Poniatowska
Photographs by Gayle Walker

UNIVERSITY OF TEXAS PRESS ⬦ AUSTIN

The Louann Atkins Temple Women & Culture Series is supported by Allison, Doug, Taylor, and Andy Bacon; Margaret, Lawrence, Will, John, and Annie Temple; Larry Temple; the Temple-Inland Foundation; and the National Endowment for the Humanities.

Copyright © 2008 by the
University of Texas Press

Printed in the United States of America
First English-language edition, 2008
Originally published as *La Doñas de Chiapas*,
©Gayle Walker and Kiki Suárez (Editorial Fray
Bartolomé de Las Casas, A. Co., 2006).

Requests for permission to reproduce material
from this work should be sent to:
    Permissions
    University of Texas Press
    P.O. Box 7819
    Austin, TX 78713-7819
    www.utexas.edu/utpress/about/
      bpermission.html

The paper used in this book meets the minimum
requirements of ANSI/NISO Z39.48-1992 (R1997)
(Permanence of Paper).

Library of Congress
Cataloging-in-Publication Data

Walker, Gayle, 1949–2006.
  Every woman is a world : interviews with
women of Chiapas / Gayle Walker and Kiki
Suárez ; edited by Carol Karasik ; foreword by
Elena Poniatowska. — 1st ed.
    p. cm. — (Louann Atkins Temple women
& culture series ; bk. 18)
  Includes bibliographical references.
  ISBN 978-0-292-71790-9 (cloth : alk. paper) —
  ISBN 978-0-292-71791-6 (pbk. : alk. paper)
  1. Women—Mexico—Chiapas—Social condi-
tions. 2. Older women—Mexico—Chiapas—
Interviews. 3. Chiapas (Mexico)—Social condi-
tions. I. Suárez, Kiki. II. Karasik, Carol. III.
Title.
  HQ1464.C44W35 2008
  305.26'209227275–dc22   2007036401

To our mothers
and
for all the doñas of Chiapas

CONTENTS

Foreword xi
Acknowledgments xv
Introduction xvii

INTERVIEWS

Guadalupe Vásquez 3
Teresa Domínguez Carrascosa 7
María del Carmen Gómez Gómez 17
Juliana López Pérez 23
Beatriz Mijangos Zenteno 29
Juana Koh 43
Merle Greene Robertson 47
María Patishtán Likanchitón 61
Carlota Zepeda Gallegos 67
Luvia Amalia Burguete Sánchez 75
Minerva Penagos Gutiérrez 87
Ana María Refugio Pineda Gómez 95
Koh Martínez 101
Dolores Rovelo Argüelles 107

Francisca Gómez López 113
Manuela Ramírez Gómez 121
Natividad Elvira Pineda Gómez 125
Sebastiana Pérez Espinoza 133
Dilery Penagos Gutiérrez 139
Micaela Díaz Díaz 145
Maruca Navarro, viuda de Alfonso 149
María Meza Girón 157
Dolores Maceiras, viuda de Suárez 161
Victoria Aguilar Hernández 169
Koh María 177
Herminia Haro Haro 183
Pascuala Pérez Gómez 191
Rosa López 197

Glossary 205
People, Customs, and Events 209
Bibliography 235
Suggested Reading 239
Author Biographies 241

The women who appear in this book come from different regions of Chiapas, from mountain towns and ranches and from hamlets in the distant rainforest. Some of them do not remember when they were born or how long they have lived on the earth; several of them are now over a hundred years old.

Their lives have not been easy. They have survived the Mexican Revolution, the Spanish influenza epidemic of 1918, religious persecution under President Plutarco Elías Calles, and times of limited opportunities in which women were marginalized.

The Mexican author Rosario Castellanos wrote about the women of Chiapas, and more than thirty years after her death her novels and poetry remain relevant. The condition of women in Chiapas has not changed much. Men still hold the reins. In *Every Woman Is a World*, Gayle Walker and Kiki Suárez honor older women, the grandmothers, who re-create history with their words.

Since childhood, these women have known how to work hard. They learned to sew, embroider, weave, and make pottery; plant the fields, grind corn, and make tortillas; cook and take care of the family. Their lives are without rest because life never stops.

The women who survived the most arduous times remember little of the past. Many suffered physical and psychological abuse, first at the hands of alcoholic fathers who drank to the point of unconsciousness. When the women married or went to live with a man, their partners treated them the same or worse.

Some of the women do not know how to read or write. The indigenous women who are not fluent in Spanish have trouble communicating with Ladinos as well as with speakers of Maya languages other than their own. When they come to town, it is a great effort for them to ask for necessities: "Could you sell me a little food?"

Micaela Díaz Díaz remembers that when she came to live in San Cristóbal, in 1977, "Indians weren't supposed to walk in the streets of San Cristóbal at night. We didn't have permission to live in town."

Some of the women have never left their homes. Others have traveled to Mexico City, Europe, and the United States. All but one returned to live out their final days in Chiapas.

Most of the women have children, grandchildren, and great-grandchildren. Others lost sons and daughters and now live alone. They go on, thanks to the sale of their textiles and ceramics and to their labors on the land. Some were truly in love with men who made them happy. Others were widowed young. A few never longed for the companionship of a man. *Mejor solita*, they say, "Better alone."

Each woman describes a critical moment in her life. María Patishtán Likanchitón was falsely jailed for being an Evangelist. Carlota Zepeda Gallegos decided to marry a controversial social activist, Erasto Urbina García, whose ideals were similar to those of the revolutionary Zapatista leader Sub-Commander Marcos. During the 1940s, followers of Erasto Urbina set fire to the ranch of Luvia Amalia Burguete Sánchez, who fought off the attack single-handedly. Later she lost her daughter to leukemia.

As a girl, Minerva Penagos Gutiérrez was badly burned with boiling water, which left prominent scars on her neck. Her parents and family stood by her, and eventually she found a loving husband. "My children have even told me, 'Look, Mama, if you didn't have your scars, you wouldn't be our mother!'"

Ana María Refugio Pineda Gómez chose not to marry and instead became a catechist, a "spiritual mother." Her sister, Natividad Elvira Pineda Gómez, devoted herself to traditional Mexican cooking: "I never learned to read or write.... But everything that I wanted to learn I just had to see once and it stayed with me. All of my recipes are in my head.... Soon I'll celebrate my one hundredth birthday, but I'm still doing the things I always did, like teaching. I will teach as long as God gives me life and I can go on."

Sebastiana Pérez Espinoza, an indigenous woman of strong character, discovered that women have the same capacity for work as men: "I knew that I was able to get what I needed all by myself. I didn't need a man to take care of me. I didn't want to have my mother's life, so I never fell in love and never got married."

Koh Martínez, a Lacandon Maya woman, was married at the age of nine. "Every time I was about to give birth, my husband would run out to the god house to pray.... [Men] are the ones with the power to talk to our gods. But women, no."

Micaela Díaz Díaz describes the general condition of women in highland Maya society: "Sometimes men hit women. Sometimes they hit too much. And that's the truth. Without a husband, there's no one to hit or yell at you."

Koh María followed the rules of conduct, passed down from mother to daughter, and accepted her destiny: "Girls are always forced to marry the men. You're always told, 'Go get married so that you can prepare the man his food.' My husband thought that women were here to make his food and to wash his clothes and to have his children."

For Maruca Navarro the phrase, "To remember is to live," means "To remember is to suffer again."

Misery and good fortune touch every life. In this book we also meet women who experienced happy marriages. Victoria Aguilar Hernández demonstrated her freedom and chose the man she married. "I never had anything but good times with him," she says. "I always had my corn and beans. And I always felt loved."

Others grew up in close-knit families. "Our way of looking at life—the rules, customs, and education that our parents gave us—has been our foundation," says Dilery Penagos Gutiérrez. "In reality, life has its challenges. It has its beautiful parts and its hard times. But overall, with a base of love and respect, even when you're confronted with especially difficult situations, you're able to get through them."

Gayle Walker and Kiki Suárez arrived in Chiapas many years ago and were captivated by its landscape and people. The history, culture, and beliefs that fascinated them (and that are mentioned in the interviews) are discussed in the final section of the book, "People, Customs, and Events."

Driven by curiosity, Gayle and Kiki decided to interview women over the age of sixty. The work was not easy. The interviews in Tzotzil, Tzeltal, and Lacandon Maya had to be done through interpreters. A number of women considered life a burden and refused to talk about it. Eventually, twenty-eight women—housewives, ranchers, businesswomen, teachers, cooks, servants, nuns, weavers, potters, and midwives—agreed to tell their stories. Gayle and Kiki are friends of many of the women in this book. They love and admire them and here present a memorable testimony of their lives.

Every Woman Is a World preserves their words and wisdom as well as their faces. Gayle and Kiki recognize the strength and sensibility of these women, who live from day to day not knowing what will happen but not frightened by tomorrow. The past is gone, and although they remember some days with joy, they probably would agree with Frida Kahlo when she exclaimed at the end of her life, "I hope I never return."

Elena Poniatowska

Everything in the universe is connected to everything else. This book grew from memories of our grandmothers, who taught us so much about love and struggle, history, people, and old age. Regret for not having listened to them more when we were young was eventually resolved in a country far from home. One day, as Kiki's mother-in-law, Dolores Maceiras, viuda de Suárez, reminisced about her childhood in San Cristóbal, the idea for this book was born.

When we began investigating the lives of older women in Chiapas we didn't know how much fun it would be, or how much work. During many pleasures and trials over the last three years, our friendship has grown stronger and deeper.

Many hearts and minds joined with us to make this book possible. First we wish to express our gratitude to our close friend and editor, Carol Karasik. Without her intelligence and expertise this book would never have come together. Carol, who is as interested in women's lives as we are, grounded us and kept us on track.

Father José Áviles, Sister Cecilia Trinidad Cruz, Luis Herrera Vásquez, Pedro Meza, and Beatriz Mijangos put us in touch with several remarkable women who gladly shared their stories with us. Other friends kindly served as translators during our interviews with indigenous women: Chan Nuk, Adriana, Flor, and Ofelia in the Lacandon community of Nahá; Lucia Hernández Girón in the Tzeltal community of Tenejapa; Marcelino Patishtán, the bright and handsome grandson of María Patishtán Likanchitón, in Chamula; and Walter "Chip" Morris, who translated the stories of Micaela Díaz Díaz and Pascuala Pérez Gómez from the Tzotzil community of San Andrés.

We also want to thank the historians Jorge Paniagua and Dr. Jan de Vos for contributing scholarly information to "People, Customs, and Events," and

Dana Burton for finding the right books. Francisco Álvarez Quiñones, Dahlia Armon, Duncan Black, Juan Blasco, Lourdes Herrasti, and Joy Whetstone provided valuable comments on the manuscript.

Special thanks to Cisco Dietz and Michael Huddleston for the generous use of their darkrooms.

We are blessed with many women friends in San Cristóbal who have helped us view women's lives in a new light: Aco Azuara, Christel Becker, Naomi Brickman, Trudi Gartmann, Pilar Gonzalez, Carolina Hernández, Marcey Jacobson, Helga Loebell, Teresa Saenz, and Flora María Sanchez. Now that we are growing old together, may the life stories of the women in this book accompany us!

Many of the stories are about bad relationships between men and women. In our own lives we are lucky to have chosen such loving mates. We are grateful to Miguel Angel Anzures and Gabriel Suárez for their patience and moral support throughout this project, and always. Kiki's husband, Gabriel, scanned and printed all the photographs and rescued us whenever we came to our wit's end at the computer. Gayle's beloved Miguel helped in ways too numerous to mention. For over twenty-five years Gayle and Miguel traveled and celebrated life to its fullest.

We are also fortunate to have extraordinary families: two strong and beautiful sisters, Gabriele Oberstenfeld and Claudia Cardinal; and a wonderful brother, Jeff Walker, who has been there through thick and thin since the day he was born. Finally we want to express our deepest appreciation to our parents, Fritz and Irmgard Oberstenfeld and Don and Jean Walker, who gave us the gift of freedom to become who we are.

This book is a collection of twenty-eight life stories of women from different socioeconomic, ethnic, and cultural backgrounds who have lived in Chiapas during the past 60 to 108 years. One woman, Merle Greene Robertson, was not born in Chiapas but dedicated a great part of her life to studying the art of the ancient Maya. We included her as an example of the many foreigners who have been enchanted by Chiapas and have decided to make their homes here.

Why did we write down these women's lives? For most of human history, young people listened to the life stories of their elders for pleasure and for guidance. The wisdom found in traditional fairy tales is the essence of the stories that countless individuals experienced and dreamed long ago. Today our mothers' and grandmothers' life stories often bore us. We look to science and the fabricated biographies of celebrities to guide us. Yet every time we listen to another person's story we immediately see that life in relation to our own. Each story helps us reevaluate and even reshape our lives.

Most life stories published in books are accounts of men who went off to discover and conquer the world. In comparison, the lives of women who stayed at home and cared for children are considered dull and mediocre. But what if the experiences of those women were regarded as a different kind of adventure, one that demanded as much courage as the exploits of heroes who ventured off to kill dragons?

Intrigued by this question, we decided to listen to the life stories of women from Chiapas, where we have lived for over twenty years. When we arrived in the colonial town of San Cristóbal de las Casas, high in the mountains of southern Mexico, we discovered a world where medieval and Maya traditions coexisted in an uneasy truce. Cold and remote, the place had resisted change for centuries. But during the past two decades, San Cristóbal has grown from

View of San Cristóbal de las Casas

a provincial town of 25,000 to a cosmopolitan city of over 150,000 citizens. Cars cause endless traffic jams. Squatters' shacks blanket the former meadows, Evangelical churches ring the hills, and, nestled by the springs at the northern edge of the valley, a Muslim mosque draws worshipers to prayer. The forests that once covered the surrounding mountains are disappearing; the crystal-clear rivers are polluted. Rampant population growth, along with a total lack of urban planning, has created all the problems and pressures of a modern city blessed with colonial charm.

Beyond San Cristóbal, hundreds of ancient Maya cities lie in ruins. Today, about one million Maya people live in traditional villages scattered across the limestone ridges of the highlands and in the vanishing jungle of the tropical lowlands. They still speak their native languages and maintain many beliefs and rituals that date back to Classic Maya civilization.

Since the Spanish Conquest, San Cristóbal has stood as a bastion of religious and political conservatism holding sway over the native population. While the upper class has profited from coffee, cocoa, mahogany, and cattle ranching, the indigenous people have endured extreme poverty. In spite of the state's natural wealth, the people of Chiapas are among the poorest in the nation.

Several times over the past few centuries the Maya have rebelled against their oppressors, but each rebellion provoked bloody reprisals that left the Maya more oppressed. The Zapatista Uprising of January 1, 1994, drew world attention to the miserable social and economic conditions of the Indian population of Chiapas. Signs of progress are few. In many communities the rift between rebel sympathizers and government supporters often erupts into violence, which has only widened the gulf between the haves and have-nots.

The Zapatista Movement is only partially responsible for challenging the status quo. Evangelical sects have caused enormous tensions in Maya communities. In San Cristóbal, Ladinos, Indians, and Mestizos encounter Mexicans from other parts of the country as well as foreigners from all over the world, some of whom have settled here and represent a permanent subculture. The proximity of so many disparate cultures and ways of thinking creates a fascinating, yet divided, community.

Such a multifaceted society seemed to be the right place for us to record women's life stories. We decided to interview women over the age of sixty because we assumed that they had witnessed extraordinary social changes in their lifetimes. How had they coped with it? Some of the women were old enough to have lived through world-altering historical events. What were their personal views of those events? No books could tell us, because there were no studies of older women in Chiapas, much less older women from diverse social backgrounds. Last but not least, we were motivated to undertake this project for personal reasons. Both of us had recently entered our fifties and were reconsidering our own stories, trying to find the meaning of our lives. Soon we would enter old age and wanted to get acquainted with it. In this sense we were looking for guidance, just like the generations of women who listened to the stories of wise women in former times.

We began by interviewing women who have played intimate roles in our lives. They came from San Cristóbal, nearby Indian communities, and the Lacandon jungle. The first interviewees led us to others.

We structured the interviews with a loose list of questions, beginning with personal memories of childhood, first loves, marriage, and motherhood. We asked the women about their work, their fears, and their thoughts about dying and death. In the end, we seldom stuck to our questions and just let the women talk. Eventually they expressed their personal concerns and revealed their perspectives on the social forces that had influenced their lives.

Eight of the women we interviewed come from prosperous or prestigious families in San Cristóbal. Although some have lost their wealth, they still maintain upper-class values. All of these women attended high school before they married and became housewives. Most achieved successful marriages. Later on, one returned to teaching, two opened businesses, and another took over the administration of her family ranch. One young widow, Maruca Navarro, worked as a typist to make ends meet, but she never recovered from her husband's tragic death. She is the only woman who did not want to have her photograph taken.

The seven Mestiza women we interviewed grew up in poor families that had abandoned the customs, dress, and language of Indian culture. Most attended a few years of grade school until economic pressures forced them to find work as maids, cooks, or laundresses. Despite stern moral strictures, several women had children out of wedlock or lived with their husbands in a common-law marriage.

The twelve indigenous women grew up in traditional Maya communities where they received no formal education. They either do not speak Spanish or speak it as a second language. Unique village customs and language separate them from one another and exclude them from the dominant culture. Yet most of these women became successful artisans whose talents have given them the wherewithal to be relatively free of the hardships that indigenous women com-

Chamula girl in front of
one of the few remaining
traditional adobe houses

monly face. Several women we interviewed were involved in the Zapatista
Movement, but without explicit permission from their leaders, they were for-
bidden to talk about political issues.

Indigenous and Mestiza women remember little about their childhoods.
The slim memories they recount are painfully similar: an absent or hard-
drinking, violent father, years of deprivation and hunger. On the other hand,
the well-to-do women recall their mothers, fathers, and siblings in great detail.
They also fondly reminisce about teenage sweethearts.

Courtship was a different matter among the poor. Most of the Maya
women we interviewed were thrust into arranged marriages when they were

barely past childhood. Surprisingly, the three Lacandon Maya women, who lived in polygamous unions, expressed few complaints about their husbands. But most indigenous women describe husbands who drank, beat them, and were unfaithful.

The women who either lost or left their husbands early in their marriages chose not to remarry. Four women never married at all. Instead of husband and family, they decided to lead a religious life, one as a catechist and two as ordained nuns. As founder of the first congregation of indigenous Catholic nuns in Chiapas, Sebastiana Pérez Espinoza dedicates her life to the health and welfare of Indian women.

Without exception, religion is a source of peace and solace in all these women's lives, even though their beliefs and practices vary widely. It is probably their deep faith that allows them to look at death with equanimity. They know that it will come eventually, but none expresses fear or fantasizes about what might or might not come afterwards. They all trust that God will help them at the final moment. Meanwhile, they enjoy what life has to offer: home, family, trips to town, or a tasty plate of beans.

These interviews tell us how twenty-eight women have dealt with the universal issues of life. Even in the worst of circumstances—hunger, violence, and the devastating loss of children—they discovered ways to surmount life's challenges. They reveal their scars, along with a remarkable resilience. Many of these life stories upset our preconceptions. Several Maya women restricted by extreme poverty, by their traditional female role, and by the complete lack of education nevertheless invented amazing opportunities for themselves out of nothing. They remind us that if we are flexible, creative, and courageous, we have many more possibilities than we think we have.

Even though biology, society, and culture shape our lives, we have some extra room for choosing how we deal with circumstances. No two human beings respond exactly the same way to life's challenges. Every woman is unique, a world unto herself. And that is what makes listening to life stories so fascinating.

Gayle Walker and Kiki Suárez, December 2005

Every Woman Is a World

Guadalupe Vásquez

Guadalupe Vásquez

I don't know how old I am, but I know I'm one of the oldest women in my town. There are many women younger than me who are all worn out. They always complain of aches and pains. I'm much older than they are and I'm doing just fine. It feels good to be an old lady and still be so strong.

I'm an Indian. I was born in Amatenango, and so was my mother, but my father came from someplace else. My father spoke Spanish, and from the time I was little I've been speaking both Spanish and Tzeltal. My parents died so many years ago that I hardly remember them. If I try hard, I can remember my mother a little. We were a lot alike.

I don't remember exactly how many brothers and sisters I had. I think there were six of us, all dead now except for me. My mother had two more daughters, my two sisters, whom she loved very, very much. But she didn't love me. I was the one she rejected.

My father used to drink and then fight with my mother. They argued a lot and even hit each other when my father came home drunk. If wives say nothing when their husbands drink, nothing happens. The husbands just pass out and everything is fine. But if the wives complain, then the hitting and fighting starts. My mother was one of those who complained.

My father died young, when I was still little. My mother never remarried. Instead, she went to live with my sister, the one she loved. A year later she died.

When I was young I would go to the mill to select the wheat for the people I worked for. Then I would bring it home to grind. I also ground the corn to make tortillas. Big ones! And I washed the clothes that people brought to me. That was my job.

I don't remember how old I was when I got married or how I met my husband, but I know I didn't love him. His family was from Teopisca, and they and my parents arranged our marriage. In fact, we never actually got married. We just lived together. But I was never happy with him.

I think I had seven or eight children, and they were all by my husband. For a while he lived with me in my house in Amatenango, but then he left me to go live with his family in Teopisca. His parents wanted me to live there too, so they came to get me. But I told them, "Why should I go if I have my own place here?" I preferred living in my own big house, the one where I was born. My children stayed with me, and I was left to look after them alone. My husband never helped me with money. I carried my children on my back, gathered firewood, harvested the corn, and made tortillas.

When my first son was born, I wanted him to be baptized. But his father said, "No, he's not going to be baptized." Well, I baptized the boy anyway! Later, when the children were old enough to go to school, the teacher came to register them. But my husband didn't want his children to have an education. He yelled at me, "Why did you put the children in school?" I said, "I'm the mother. I take care of them, and they're going to school if I say so!" We had a big fight over that. It made me feel so good to have my children in school.

My husband never looked after his children. He didn't buy them clothes or schoolbooks or medicine when they got sick. So, like that, I brought them up—washing clothes and cutting wood with a hatchet. I worked hard.

My children are all grown up now. They have children of their own. And their children have children! But I don't see them very often. My three daughters work in San Cristóbal. My first daughter never married, so she lives alone. One son lives in Amatenango and sometimes he and his family come to my house. "Oh, we came to visit," they say. "We came for the tortillas." And then they run to the *comal* and devour all my tortillas. Other times they visit when there's a fiesta. That's when all the family comes, and those days are happy ones. They love me then.

For many years I lived alone in my house, but now my youngest son is here with me. He takes care of me, and I appreciate it so much. He's a good boy and I love him the most. He's a sweet and good man. He hasn't married yet because he's waiting until I pass away. He works hard. Once he went all the way to Mexico City, but then he came back to me. Now he tends the cornfield, washes our clothes, and cooks. He's a sensitive man. After all the years that I lived alone, I'm much better off now with my son. I don't have to buy corn anymore, because we have our own. We have enough of everything.

My life has been bitter at times. It has been difficult and sad, but I'm happy anyway. A while back I got sick, but the people of Amatenango looked after me and I got better. I never think about dying. It doesn't scare me at all. When God wants, he can take me. I live day by day and I'm still strong.

I've always planted flowers in my garden. When I'm able, I don't stay at home. Several times a week I say to myself, "Oh yes, today I'll go to San Cristóbal." Then I get on the bus and go to town to sell my flowers. I also like to go to mass, because the church is bigger and nicer in San Cristóbal.

People really like me. Yes, both in Amatenango and in San Cristóbal. After I sell my flowers I go visiting. When I pass by on the street, people call out to me, "Doña Lupita! Come sit and talk to me for a while." Then I go to the market where people like me too. I have lots of friends. That's why I come here so often. I almost never go to Teopisca. I like it all right, but the people aren't as friendly as they are in Amatenango and San Cristóbal.

You bought some flowers from me, so I'm finished working. Now I'm going to the market. One of my daughters is waiting for me there, and later I'm going to see one of my friends. I don't remember her name, but she's my friend. So that's it for today. Now I'm going visiting. . . .

Teresa Domínguez Carrascosa

Teresa Domínguez Carrascosa

I'm ninety-six years old and have spent my whole life in this house on Real de Guadalupe Street. I've lived here since I was born, almost one hundred years ago, and the house was already more than one hundred years old when my father bought it from his aunt.

My father had an extremely fussy disposition. My brothers and I always had to behave ourselves because if we didn't, our father would become angry with us. When we'd hear him opening the door, we'd say, "Papa's here!" and immediately be on our best behavior. Yes, he had a terrible personality. We were always afraid of him. We never touched his things because we didn't want him to yell at us. There were never any tender or loving moments with my father.

But my mother was pure love, always sweet and gentle. I remember many close, beautiful moments with her. I also got along very well with my three brothers. Since I was the youngest, everyone loved me. My father warned my brothers, "Take care of your little sister!" Our childhood was in part happy and in part sad, like the rest of my life has been.

I lived through the Mexican Revolution and remember that all of us were terribly afraid. There were constant threats that General Venustiano Carranza's men were going to seize the plaza and that the soldiers would ransack the houses. I would eavesdrop on the adults' conversations and become very frightened. All of those awful rumors made my father extremely nervous, and he would sink into an ugly mood.

At the time, General Pineda was in control of San Cristóbal. Everyone here loved him because he was an admirable man. But one of Pineda's officers, a man named Argüelles, wasn't guarding the entrances to the town properly. Carranza's men poured through La Ventana Pass and invaded the city. Pineda was a serious man and knew how to wage war, but he couldn't defend the plaza and finally had to flee. The men who were running with him were our relatives, our friends, many respectable men from Tabasco.

When the troops were fleeing, my father shouted, "Bring water and tortillas!" I remember standing at the window of our house handing food to the troops as those poor men ran to who knows where.

Carranza's men entered the city cautiously, because they feared that Pineda's army would make a surprise attack. But you see, General Pineda's parents lived in the city, and he was afraid that Carranza would hold them hostage. And so Pineda's army spent the whole night watching and waiting on Guadalupe Hill. In the end, nothing happened to the parents, and Pineda and his troops retreated to their headquarters in Ocosingo. Carranza's forces took possession of San Cristóbal, but his soldiers never looted the houses. I was too young to remember all that happened, but eventually the situation calmed down.

The Spanish influenza epidemic arrived in 1918. They said the virus came from the United States. It was such a frightful thing! In every house in town, people took to their beds, and there was no one to take care of them. The doors were kept wide open day and night so that if by chance a doctor walked by and wanted to perform an act of charity, he would be able to enter the house to attend the sick. No one was afraid of robbery because even the thieves were sick in bed.

When someone died, the family would wrap the body in a sheet and load the corpse onto a wagon pulled by oxen. Indians drove the wagon. Who knows who paid them, or how. We had a dear friend, Alfonso Coello, who was very charitable. He would pass by the houses to see if anyone inside had died, and if they had, he would take them out and wrap the body in paper or in a straw mat and then set the body out on the sidewalk to be picked up. I would listen to the noise of the wagon ... clack-ka-clack-ka ... when it passed by the house. The streets were deserted.

One day my mother sent me out to buy food from the few people who were still selling in the market. I was the only one on the streets. On the corner

I heard the sound of the wagon and I stopped to watch as it went by. The bodies were piled up, some with their heads hanging out the back, others with their feet dangling out. And one of those feet wore a red sock. I'll never forget that sight. It was horrible!

In the house on the corner, Doctor Velasco died. Over on the next street, Doctor Durango died too. When our neighbor passed away, I ran into the street and saw four men carrying out a coffin painted red. The Indians had painted it however they could. There was loss of life throughout the whole town. Big pits were dug where all the bodies were buried.

In my house everyone was sick in bed except for me. And when everyone was more or less well, I fell ill. But I didn't get terribly sick and was only in bed for about four days. A cousin of mine brought me raisins to eat. Finally, the people who made it through the epidemic got out of bed, but now they were dying of hunger. Luckily, everyone in my family survived.

When I was young I never wasted my time. I loved school. I've spent my whole life studying. I attended a small school that my cousin started, and later went to La Enseñanza School where I put my heart and soul into my studies. I followed to a T all the advice the principal gave me, so there was never a complaint about me.

Later I decided to become a teacher and attended the first Normal School in San Cristóbal. The main college in Tuxtla Gutiérrez objected to the new school because there had always been rivalry between the two towns. But our director, Miss María Adelina Flores, stuck to all the rules of pedagogy, and the school turned out to be wonderful.

Because our class was to be the first to graduate, we studied constantly. The college in Tuxtla put every obstacle in our path to keep us from graduating. But our director told us, "Children, in the name of God, carry on!" They weren't able to stop us, and we accomplished everything that María Adelina had hoped for.

Four of us completed the program. But in order to graduate, we had to ride on horseback from San Cristóbal to Tuxtla to take the final exams. My father, as difficult as he was, had to let me go, but he insisted that my older sister accompany me. Since she had never been away from home, the trip was to serve as an outing for her. It was a day's trip from here to Ixtapa, where we spent the night with a family we knew, sleeping on a bed of pine straw on their living room floor. Then we spent another whole day of travel. I was nervous because I didn't know how they might torture us at the exam in Tuxtla. Since they didn't want a new school in San Cristóbal, they were surely going to make our exam as difficult as possible. They tested us subject by subject, first theory and then practice. Also, we had to come up with solutions to certain social problems. The Indians were beginning to cause trouble around that time, so the professors asked me to suggest practical ways on how to "de-fanaticize" them. We all finished the exam with great success.

In Tuxtla we became good friends with Don Bernardo Félix, the father of María Félix, the famous movie actress. I don't remember what political position he had there. One night he invited us, together with other young women from San Cristóbal, to a party. We sang to guitar music. It was a joyful affair.

The government certified our studies, and I became a professor at the college I had attended in San Cristóbal.

I met my husband here in this house. He was a relative of ours who had come to visit my father. His name was Juan, and he was an agronomist from Pichucalco. One day my father called my sister and me and said, "Look, this is Juan." And then and there it all began. We fell in love, and one day Juan came to the house and said, "I'm going to ask your father for your hand in marriage. We'll see what he says." Well, my father said that we could be married whenever we wanted; and we did, with his total approval. My father was the kind of man who would never have allowed me to marry anyone but a relative.

I was twenty-nine years old when we married, but I had other boyfriends before Juan. They brought me many serenades. But when the marimbas began to play, my father became angry. I never had the opportunity to talk with any of the young men who brought me music. Not a single opportunity for even one chat! My father detested those serenades and would lock himself in his room and us in ours. There were many serenades and, yes, sometimes I fell in love. I was so impressed by those young men. Oh, they were so handsome!

Once I fell in love with a serious young man who was a notary public. Now I don't remember his name. I was never given the chance to talk with him. He never even had the opportunity to declare himself to me. Every day I went to mass at the Church of San Nicolás and he would be there. But I was so afraid that my father would see us talking that I clung to my aunt's arm so that the young man couldn't approach me. Every day we saw each other in church, and every Saturday night he brought me a serenade with marimba. I don't even know if I felt real affection for him or if it was just curiosity. He would wait on the corner every morning to see if I would come to talk with him. And so one day, out of all those days, I went alone, and out he came from his hiding place to speak to me. But I said, "I'm afraid to talk to you because my parents might see us."

"But your parents aren't around," he answered.

"I know," I said, "but I feel as if they will appear at any moment."

And so perhaps there could have been someone else besides Juan whom I would have liked more, but with my father the way he was, it was impossible. And now I know that with the other men I wouldn't have been as happy.

Juan was a well-bred man and was always looking after me. Once he told me, "I didn't marry you because I was looking for a cook." He was a gentle and loving man, very different from my father. He wouldn't allow even a rose petal to fall on me.

He was a widower eighteen years older than I and knew much about life. His wife had died seven years before, and he had seven children. The oldest two were already doctors when we met.

We were married quietly because, during the 1930s, there was heavy religious persecution. At night the priest's house was under steady government surveillance, to make sure that no one secretly did something they shouldn't.

My future husband was a friend of the governor who was persecuting the church. One day the governor asked him, "Are you planning on marrying in the church?" And Juan answered him, "Yes, even if you get furious with me,

I'm going to be married in the church or else not be married at all! Do whatever you want!"

We talked secretly with the priest and decided to marry at nine o'clock in the morning, because at that hour no one would be watching. I carried my wedding dress in a basket, and when I arrived at the priest's house, he showed me to a room where I changed my clothes. My mother and I went alone. My father refused to come because he didn't want to see me dressed as a bride. It was just too much for him. He was such a strange man.

Juan arrived with a very dear friend who would be the witness for the wedding. Then we went to the priest's little chapel and he married us. After the ceremony I changed out of my wedding dress and we left the priest's house one by one, so that no one in the street would see us leave together. I left with my mother, and then Juan came out and went to the hotel where we would meet later. We couldn't have a party because then everyone would know about the sin we had committed.

A month later we had the civil ceremony. We waited that long so that no one would realize we had already been married in the church. The ceremony was held here in this hallway. Here was where my parents had been married, and here is where the banquet table stood.

All of my friends were at my civil wedding. The judge was all dressed up in a new black suit. Many people from the government came, because Juan moved in those circles. But my father never left his room because he didn't want to see me as a bride, and so my brother gave me away. After the ceremony the waiters served glasses of champagne and there was marimba music. My mother said, "Juan may be a widower, but you surely aren't!"

We wanted everything to be over quickly. I danced, we all danced, and everybody was happy, and then there was another song on the marimba and another glass of champagne. I changed into my traveling suit and we went to Comitán on our honeymoon. Everything was simple and pleasant. First we lived in the house across the street. But five months later my father died, and we moved back into this house.

I lived with my husband for thirty-five years, until he passed away. We had four children. They were very well behaved and we never had problems with any of them. We lived here with my mother and with Demetria, the woman who raised her and whom we loved as a second mother. We lived very peacefully and happily and never had any quarrels or arguments. The saddest part of that era of my life was when our eighteen-month-old baby son died of intestinal complications. Losing a child is very, very hard for a mother.

I wanted Juan's seven children to live with us. When he first proposed to me, I said, "No, no, I don't want to be responsible for a bunch of kids!" And he answered me, "My children won't be living with us." But after we were married, we went to visit them in Tuxtla and I saw that his two youngest girls weren't doing well. They were seven and nine years old and were living with their aunt, but it seemed that no one cared if they were there or not.

"Look, Juancho," I told my husband, "those two girls shouldn't be here. I'm going to bring them with us to San Cristóbal. They're so young, and if they stay here, they'll be ruined." So the two girls came to live in our house.

I am very satisfied with all of Juan's children and with my own. His children helped me a lot when mine were small. I never tried to force myself on them, and so we all got along. I enjoy them even now, and when they visit San Cristóbal they come to give me a hug. "How are we going to forget you when you were a second mother to us," they tell me.

I didn't work until one of my sons wanted to go to school in Mexico City and we didn't have enough money to send him. That's when I began teaching again. I enjoyed practicing my profession. Juan didn't want me to teach, but there wasn't any alternative. So I worked until it was time for me to retire.

The death of my husband was the saddest thing in my life. Juan suffered a stroke six years before his death and was an invalid from then on. We would put him out in his wheelchair to sit on the patio. Since he had always read a lot, he wanted us to leave him an open book and a magnifying glass. But by then he didn't assimilate things well. The magnifying glass would stay in one spot on the page, and when the sun came out, the paper would burn. He couldn't speak other than to say "yes" and "no." Those six years were hard, and finally he passed away.

It's been twenty-one years since my husband died. His passing has been sad for me, but life gives us no choice. Now I live here with my daughter, who is divorced. My whole life has been in this house where we live quietly without anyone bothering us.

What I enjoy most each day are my prayers. Every day I entrust my children to God. I used to like to read a lot and to do handcrafts. I've made many beautiful pieces, but now I don't see well. I can't write or watch television either. I try to listen to it, but I don't hear well. I pass my days a little bored.

I used to go out to many gatherings and dances, Christmas parties and *posadas*. Now I go to bed at six o'clock. I remember those parties, but I'm satisfied with what once was. We all must come to our end. When I think about death I say, "Lord, you gave us life and you will take it from us. Please make it sweet."

María del Carmen Gómez Gómez

María del Carmen Gómez Gómez

My family lived in a beautiful place in the country, on the slopes of Huitepec Mountain. I was born there about seventy-five years ago, the first of seven children. From a very young age I carried around my younger brothers and sisters and helped my mother wash clothes. Our family always suffered because we were so poor.

Liquor was always a part of our lives. My father was a laborer who worked in the market for ten or twenty cents a day. He would go off to work in the morning, but then he wouldn't return home right away because he would go out to drink. When my father did come home, he would yell at us, and then he would hit my mother. I would gather my brothers and sisters and we would run out to hide in the forest. It was a thick forest, and we were scared, but we were more afraid of our father. After my father went to bed, my mother would call out to us, "Come back inside, my babies! Where have you gone? Come home and eat!" And so we'd go back home. By that time it was late at night and we were hungry.

What I felt most toward my father was fear. Sometimes when he came home drunk, my mother would hide from him. If we didn't tell him where she was hiding, he would beat us with his belt. And it would hurt! We would tell him, "We'll look for her, Papa! We're going right now to look for her, so please don't hit us!" We always tried to protect our mother. We would say, "Please, Papa, don't hit Mama anymore!" And if he promised, we would go out to look for her.

When I was twelve or thirteen years old I left home. I told my father, "Even though you don't want me to go, I'm going to look for work so that I can help to buy food. I'll give you part of my pay but only if you promise not to hit Mother anymore. If you do, then who knows who will help the family? If you hit Mother again, I won't help you at all. My baby sisters don't even know how to make tortillas!"

"I promise not to hit her again," my father said.

My brothers were older by then, and I asked them to take care of our mother. "Yes," they said, "we'll protect her."

So I went to work for a family on Comitán Street in downtown San Cristóbal. The husband was a lieutenant in the army. They made me carry around their children, just as I had at home. I washed their clothes but never learned anything about cooking. I wasn't any good in the kitchen. They treated me well, and I worked for them for several years. But my mother fell ill and I wanted to go home to take care of her. The family I worked for begged me, "Please don't leave us!" They even went to my house to talk with my parents. But I wanted to take care of my mother, and eventually she got well.

By the time my mother was healthy again the family I had been working for had moved away, and so I went to take care of another baby in another family. But I didn't learn a thing about pots and pans at that house either. The wife cooked the food, and I washed, cleaned, and cared for the children. I enjoyed it. What else was I to do? I liked the pay, and with the grace of God, I had found another good family.

One day they said, "We would like to go to your house!" Each Thursday I went to visit my mother, and so I told her, "The people I work for want to come to visit."

"What?" asked my mother, surprised.

"Yes, this Sunday," I said.

"Well, all right," my mother said. "I'll be waiting for them."

There wasn't a road through the woods to our house, but the couple came to meet my mother anyway. I don't remember what they brought or what else we ate, but my mother gave them beans and tortillas. We didn't even have a chicken to offer them.

While I was working with that family, I found a boyfriend. We met when I was fifteen and he was twenty-five. I didn't want to get married, so I told him, "No thanks. I'm not interested."

But his parents went to talk to mine, and they liked the idea. His parents were already quite old. When I got home one day, they were all sitting there. His parents said, "You're coming to live with us."

"How can I go?" I asked. "How will I take care of myself?"

My future husband answered me, "Don't worry, you won't have to work anymore. My mother will make the tortillas from now on."

And my parents said, "Look, dear, the boy says that he loves you. Don't you want to marry him?"

I said, "Oh, I don't know. No! Later he'll just hit me!"

I wasn't in love with him, but I finally gave in. "Okay, but let me see. Give me six months to decide." The time passed and he began to drink, so I said, "No. Better not!"

But he was insistent and told me, "Let's do it!" He tricked me into marrying him. Even though our wedding took place in the cathedral, I felt very sad. I was thinking, "Now it's my turn to have the same life as my mother's!"

So my husband and I started our life together, but I wasn't happy. I quit working and went to live with my in-laws. But his mother didn't make the tortillas like they said she would. That was a lie! At home my mother ground corn on a metate, then washed it and ground it again until the cornmeal was fine. My mother-in-law didn't do it that way because she didn't know how.

My husband treated me badly. He hit me. And before long I began to feel strange and weak and didn't feel like working. I was pregnant. I asked my mother, "What's wrong with me?"

"That's life," she told me. "Now you won't be alone anymore."

When the baby was about to arrive, my husband went to get my mother, who knew how to birth babies. She was a midwife. I had no injections, nothing but a salve that she rubbed on my belly. Then she said, "All right, this is it! Squat down here, my daughter!"

The birth was difficult. I just wanted to die. We had no drinks or oils, nothing but an herb called chamomile. I fainted from weakness. It's hard having children, especially the first one. The other children's births weren't so difficult, and the girls were no trouble at all. I had four boys and two girls. I had my daughter Candelaria all alone because my husband had gone to get my mother. I was strong enough to do it myself, even though I couldn't cut the cord. I waited for my mother to come to do that. And she was with me when my last boy was born. Luckily, all my children were born healthy. Mother bathed each one with soap and water, rubbed them with her hands to warm them, and then dressed them in their tiny clothes.

I don't remember anything good about my relationship with my husband. He was no good, just like my father. When he came home, my children and I would hide in the forest. Sometimes he worked, chopping wood, and then would go around selling it. But there was no money in that. Two or three stacks of firewood would only buy a little beans and a bag of sugar!

I would carry firewood on my back, with the baby sitting on top of the stack, and would sell a load for twenty-five cents in order to buy a little food. My mother-in-law didn't work. She just looked after her sheep. My father-in-law sold firewood too, but then he'd go off to a ranch where he had another wife and family.

I told him, "Come to your senses! How can you have another wife, old man? My poor mother-in-law is here in the house waiting for you."

But she had to accept it. They were always mad at each other. Oh, women do nothing but suffer!

We hardly had anything to eat. Sometimes we just had a little *atole*. We never had chicken. We never had soup or anything tasty. Later, when my sons were old enough to work, they would bring me a chicken or a little money. They would always ask, "How are you and Papa doing?"

"Just the same," I would say. "Just the same."

One of my sons went to live in San Felipe, just outside San Cristóbal. The youngest one took his wife north to Aguascalientes where she had a brother who was a carpenter. One day he told me, "I'm going, Mother." He was a little drunk at the time.

"Please don't go!" I said. "You can work here." But he went anyway and left me crying. I haven't heard from him since, and it's been four years now.

My sister died and then my father. He had quit drinking so much and had stopped hitting my mother. With time, my brothers died and my mother too.

I still have two brothers, but they don't care about me. They don't speak to me or come to see me. They're a little strange. We had problems over the land my father left me so that my children could build a house. When my mother died, my brothers took my land away from me. My husband said, "Why do you want so much land when we already have a little? Good God! Why are you crying?"

I was sick of the arguing. I just said, "They can have it! I don't care!" Now they don't speak to me.

I still live with my husband. A few years ago he had a stroke. He's paralyzed—after chasing and hitting me for so long! He can't drink anymore or even walk. He just lies in bed and eats. I wash his clothes, clean him every day, and take care of him. I hardly ever go out of the house. We live alone together up in the forest.

Life gives us such sadness. Sometimes I say, "What am I going to do?" I have good days and bad days. The best days are when I have something good to eat. That makes me happy. The days when there's nothing much to eat I feel sad and say, "Oh, dear God, please help me find some food!" Sometimes I don't even have twenty cents to my name. Other times my daughter Chelo brings me some soup.

I have sweet, beautiful grandchildren who come to visit me and bring me things. That's when I'm happy. But sometimes there's nothing. Nothing.

When I think about death, I say, "What am I going to do? Who will stay here in my house?" I'm not afraid of dying, but I feel sad that I'll leave my house alone. I don't want to die because I don't want to leave my children and grandchildren. I pray to God to take away this sadness.

Juliana López Pérez

Juliana López Pérez

I was born here in this house in Amatenango seventy-three years ago. My mother was a potter, like all the women in Amatenango. My father, like all the men here, worked in the fields. Our custom is that men never make pottery. It always was and still is just the women, even the very old ones, who work with clay. My mother's cousin, Alberto, is the only man who has ever been a potter. There's never been a man like him in Amatenango. He's different. He wanted to work, but not in the fields like the other men. Ever since Alberto was a young boy he was interested in working with clay. There was never a problem with that. Nobody cared. Nobody gossiped. But being a potter is women's work. By the time my sisters and I were twelve years old we knew how to coil the pots by hand, fire them in the pits—everything.

Now we take our pots and water jugs to San Cristóbal in a truck. But when I was young, we carried our pots on horseback. One horse could carry twelve big jugs. We would leave very early and travel all day long. Around five o'clock in the afternoon we would deliver our pottery to the stores and then turn around and head back home. At night, when we were about halfway home, we would stop to sleep by the side of the road.

Back then, we sold a water jug for ten cents. It took so much time and work to make just one jug, and we sold it so cheaply. Our work didn't bring in enough for us to eat. And since my father couldn't plant enough corn to feed my six brothers and sisters, we had to look for corn wherever we could find it. We'd carry pots and jugs to the lowlands and try to exchange them for food. When people bought our pots and jugs, we'd have corn and beans. But mostly we went hungry. Sometimes there was just enough corn for tortillas in the morning. At night we would have nothing to eat. Sometimes a man in Teopisca sold us beans with bugs in them. The corn was just too expensive for us to buy.

My father was a good man. He didn't treat my mother too badly. My parents got along well, and even though we were so poor and suffered so much, my mother was happy. My father drank a lot, but he wasn't violent. He would just fall asleep when he got drunk. He would go to the mountains with the other men, and they would drink and sleep up there. Sometimes they would hunt for a rabbit, an opossum, or an armadillo. Then my father would come home with food for us.

My mother was very sweet and good. That's why on the Day of the Dead I always remember her by taking flowers to the cemetery. She left me this plot of land. She left me my own big house. My mother taught me how to work so that I could support myself.

I did have a man for a while. Yes, I got married when I was thirteen years old. My husband, Mariano, was around twenty. He and his family came to ask for me. But my mother didn't ask me if I wanted to marry him. She just gave me to him. So I married him and moved to his mother's house. But Mariano was very, very bad. He hit me a lot and I was afraid of him. I was angry that I was forced to marry Mariano. That anger, I think, eventually made me sick with the gall bladder.

My husband died not long after we were married. I was happy when he died. If he had lived, I don't know what would have happened to me. Maybe I would have died instead of him.

After my husband was gone, I came back to live in my parents' house and started working again with my mother. I told her, "I'm not going to live with a man anymore."

By then my father had a grandson and a nephew, and they began to plant the fields together. Little by little my father's cornfield grew. Things got better, and we had more corn and beans. When my sister married, things got even better.

It was around that time that June Nash came to visit me. She worked as an anthropologist. I began to talk with her just like we're talking now. She was really interested in history. We talked together every day. Then she took me to San Cristóbal where she was doing translations. I'd come back to Amatenango for the fiestas and music. But I lived and worked with June, and she fed me. I entered a different world in San Cristóbal. I didn't know anything, but I would hear what people were saying and I'd remember it all in my head. Everything there was fascinating to me.

June was writing a book, and she decided to take me with her to the United States. I was around twenty years old then. We traveled by car for nine days from San Cristóbal to New York. We didn't drive at night. That's why it took so long to get there. I was always thinking, "Yes, yes, we're almost there!" But there was always another day of travel. I was thinking, "We must be close, very close." But, no, we weren't close yet. It was so far! And then when we finally arrived at the coast and I first saw the ocean, I thought, "I'm lost. I'm really lost!" I didn't speak any English, just Spanish, and not much of that. I felt very, very strange there in the United States.

I stayed for three or four months in Connecticut. June worked at the university, and I went to school with her. I would talk to the students and ask them the names for different things. But those kids didn't know anything. Sometimes I would go out in the streets by myself. One afternoon I went out, turned the corner, and walked to where the school should have been. But I took the wrong turn and got lost. Really lost! I looked and looked for the school. Which way should I go? I had a slip of paper with my address on it, and I showed it to people, but no one helped me. Around five o'clock in the afternoon I stopped a bus and showed the paper to the driver. He told me, "I'll drop you off right in front of your house." I thought, "How wonderful!" June was worried and was about to call the police. In the United States I wore my traditional dress, so it wouldn't have been hard for the police to find me!

In New York I enjoyed eating cakes and going to parties. One day we'd go to a Chinese restaurant and another day to a Japanese restaurant. They'd say, "Let's go try this food today." I loved it. But I gained lots of weight and came home fat.

Later I went to Washington for a year to take care of a family's children. I traveled to Colorado and to Minnesota too. I made about five or six trips in all. I went in summer and in winter. It was cold in the winter, and there was so much snow. I had never seen snow before! I had lots of clothes on, but I still didn't want to go outside. So cold! The lady I worked for bought me a heavy coat, gloves, boots, and a cap. I went out like that on Halloween and on Christmas Day.

I never learned to speak English. It was just too hard. I understood it some, but I couldn't speak it. The American men were handsome, and they always respected me, but I never fell in love with one. It's better to be alone. Alone, I can go wherever I want. Nobody scolds me. No one tells me what to do. I'm happy by myself. I never wanted to have children because I felt they would trap me. If I had children, I couldn't have gone out to parties with the anthropologists!

When I returned to San Cristóbal I got a job teaching children how to make things with clay. First I taught kindergarten, and then for many years I worked with older children. I went to all the parties the gringos gave, those of the hippies and those of the anthropologists. People liked me. I'm interesting.

When I finally quit teaching, around ten years ago, I returned to live and work in Amatenango. I left the life in San Cristóbal, with all of its interesting people, behind. I'm tired of that now.

I'm very happy living here with my sister, even though I have almost nothing. My sister gives me food. We live well. My brother-in-law and all of his sons work. Look at all the sacks of corn we have! They're stacked from the floor to the ceiling. And we have lots of beans. With the money my sister and I earn from the sale of our pots, we buy a little meat. We don't eat meat every day, just once a week, on Saturday or Sunday. There's not the misery I suffered when I was young.

One day an artist came here and took a photograph of me making a dove out of clay. Then he made an enormous statue of me. It's sitting on the Pan-American Highway at the entrance to San Cristóbal. Now the statue is there for everyone to see. But they didn't pay me anything. Not a thing. Later the governor's wife came to see me, and I asked her about my pay. She told me that the artist, who was her friend, had died, and so there was no one who could pay me. But, yes, it's an honor. In a way I don't like to have my statue there while I'm still alive. If I were dead, it would be different. But others tell me that I'm famous because of my statue. There are people who tell me that it's even better that I'm still alive to be able to see it. They say that my portrait, something of me, will be left behind after I'm gone.

I'm still doing what I've done all my life. Every day I make five or six little pots. I used to work from early morning until eight o'clock at night. Nowadays I don't work so hard. And my work has changed a lot. Now people want my small pots. Before, they mostly asked for water jugs and jars and flowerpots. A few of my flowerpots are still in Na Bolom. My mother's work is still there too. Something special that I'm proud of are my clay figures of doves, which no one had ever made before. Now they're very popular.

There have been many changes in Amatenango since I was young. Our houses used to be made of adobe and straw. There was always mud everywhere and the town was dirty. Now the houses are made of cement block. I like them much better. The town is clean and the highway is paved. I enjoy many of the changes. That's why I'm calm and happy. Everything is better than it used to be, not just in my life but for everyone here.

When I think about it, my life has been a little strange. Even so, if I had to do it all over again, I wouldn't change it. I'm very happy with the life I've lived. I've done just about everything. Now I spend my time thinking about how peaceful my life is. I'm through traveling all over the world.

Beatriz Mijangos Zenteno

Beatriz Mijangos Zenteno

I grew up in a big, pretty house by the river in Bochil. I remember it so well. My mother was from Bochil, and my father was from San Cristóbal. He studied in the seminary but later changed his mind and married my mother. I was born on March 14, 1932.

Mother used to be a teacher and a seamstress. Every morning she would go off to teach at the school and then come home in the afternoon to do all the work in the house. We had a bakery, and we made candles too. Really, we did a little of everything. My father was a professor and later was named school supervisor.

I remember when we used to travel from Bochil to San Cristóbal to visit my grandfather. My mother went on horseback, sitting sidesaddle, because that's the way women rode back then. My brother, the baby, traveled in his cradle. My brothers and sisters and I rode in a chair, yes, sitting in a chair with a big awning over it. An Indian from the village of Naranjo carried us on his back. That's how he made money. It was his job. He must have been very strong because it was a two-day walk to San Cristóbal.

When I was seven years old my parents separated, and we stayed with our mother in Bochil. But one day my aunt, my father's sister, came to see if we wanted to visit our father. And, of course, we did. We loved our mother, but we never went back to live with her. She stayed in Bochil and never came to look for us. How could she have given us away like that? Even my little brother, the baby!

I was seven when we moved to San Cristóbal. My sisters, Dilery and Chelo, were five and three. We lived on Tapachula Street, number thirty-five. My father was wonderful, a really good person. He brought another mother for us, and she treated us very well, just like a real mother. We loved her very much. We all had head lice then, and she would sit us on her lap. My head in her lap, my sister's head in mine, and my brother's head on Dilery. We made a chain of bodies. Then she would clean us. Yes, she was very good to us, and we all love her to this day.

I really never knew my real mother. I didn't see her again until my youngest sister married. We were in the town of Tapachula, waiting for the train to take us back to San Cristóbal. Someone said, "Here comes your mother. That lady who is looking at you. It's your mother. There she is!" I didn't even recognize her. After that, I never saw her again until she died on September nineteenth last year. In all those years, she never looked for us.

When I was young I hated school. I was more interested in trees and flowers. And cooking. Eventually cooking became my profession. But my father put me in the preparatory school that used to be in front of the cathedral. The school was in a beautiful building with a tile roof. But I escaped from there. No, I just couldn't do it. I really hated school.

My father told me, "You must have a career, because your future is ahead of you." I thought that things would always stay the way they were. I never thought about the future. First I decided to ask my aunt to teach me to bake bread. But instead, she put me to washing pots and pans. All I wanted to do was to make bread. So I said, "No, I don't want to do this. I don't like working in the bakery."

My father always gave in to my whims, because he knew me well. So then I thought, "I'll be a seamstress like my mother." So they sent me to trade school to learn to make patterns—and to do mathematics!

"Oh, I can't do mathematics," I said. "I can't add or divide!"

My father told me about a woman who lived on the corner who could teach me to cut patterns. But my aunt said to him, "Why are you going round and round about this? The girl just needs a spanking. Either she should go to school or learn a trade."

Again I told my father that I wanted to be a seamstress. I asked a friend to teach me, and she told me to do this thing and another, and little by little I would learn.

I decided to make a dress for my aunt, who was very thin and tiny, like me. I folded the fabric into four parts before I cut, but the waist came out enormous. Now they were really going to scold me! Where would I get the money to pay for that?

My friend said, "Yes, dear, I told you what to do and you just went and ruined it right away. I can't fix it for you now. I have too much work to do. But in that big house over there, the one called Na Bolom, there's a woman who's a seamstress. She can cut by sight, without a measuring tape."

I went and knocked on the door and out came a lady with a scarf wound around her head and a shawl wrapped tightly around her shoulders. The weather was cold and rainy, I remember. "Good morning," I said. "Is Doña Vila in?"

"That's me. Can I help you?" she asked, and then led me into the old kitchen, which had a huge, warm bread oven. She asked my name, and I told her it was Beti. When I explained my problem to her, she said, "Yes, I'll fix your dress for you, but not until the day after tomorrow. My bosses are coming in today from the jungle."

At that very moment Doña Trudi Blom came into the kitchen, screaming! She was tall and thin, dressed in green, with a red scarf tied in her hair. Oh, what a beautiful woman!

Behind her was Frans, her husband. Everyone called him Don Pancho. At once I tried to hide from him. You see, I used to come and play with the doorbell, which still exists to this day. Of course, Don Pancho recognized me and said, "Ay, I know this little girl."

He started scolding me, and I was so scared that I thought I would die. He was a gringo, or at least I thought so because he had pale skin and blue eyes. And the lady was so elegant.

She pointed to me and asked, "Who is this child? Who does she belong to?" Doña Trudi had such a harsh way of speaking sometimes. But she just kept staring at me. I had big eyes and she liked them, I think, because she began to sing "La Malagueña": *What pretty eyes you have beneath those two brows. . . ."*

I tried to hide from her, but she kept staring. "No!" she ordered. "Look at me. Your eyes are so pretty."

Don Pancho scolded me, "You're the one who plays with my doorbell, aren't you? What's your name?"

I was so frightened I started to cry. So they took me to the dining room and sat me down. Don Pancho looked sternly at me and said, "That bell is not a toy. If you play with it again, I'm going to cut your hands off!" He was so mad!

After they calmed down, they said, "We would like to adopt a little girl so that we can have a daughter. Think about it and then come back to let us know. But don't play with the doorbell! Stay and wait until someone answers the door."

When my father found out that I was spending time at Trudi's house, he came to get me. I cried for him to let me stay. Doña Trudi said to him, "Why don't you let her stay here for a week or two?" And like that, little by little, my father became accustomed to my living there.

Back then, I was very thin and tiny. I didn't look as old as I really was. I looked very young. Don Pancho would put me on his shoulders and play with me as if I were a little girl. I had long, long hair that Trudi combed and braided for me.

For my fifteenth birthday, Doña Trudi let me choose whether I wanted to go to San Miguel de Allende, to Mexico City, or to the Lacandon jungle. I chose the jungle because it sounded so pretty. But when Trudi told me we were going in an airplane, I cried, "No! Let's walk instead." Trudi laughed so hard that she rolled on the floor, because, you see, it was so far away—days and days. It would have taken weeks to get there on foot. But I didn't want to go by plane. No. I was afraid of flying. Finally she said to me, "Look, we'll go on horseback, then."

We left San Cristóbal with eighteen horses that carried all our provisions, like rice and corn. There was Trudi and me and an American woman named Anita Holmes. How wonderful! I'll never forget it. It was my fifteenth birthday, and it was marvelous.

Oh, I remember that first day as if it were yesterday. I never tired of riding horseback. The men who were in charge of the horses went ahead, cutting a path with their machetes. How thick the jungle was! But they knew the way. Doña Trudi rode in front, as always. Then came Doña Anita behind her, and then me. We crossed many rivers. There were so many streams, all swollen with rain. And so many animals! We saw thousands of birds—parrots, toucans, peacocks, wild turkeys, chachalacas, and *cojolites*, which sing so prettily. There were wild boar everywhere and deer too. And snakes, lots of snakes. We even saw a jaguar, all black and sleek.

At night we stopped to sleep in hammocks under the trees. The men cooked for us. They built huge bonfires to keep the animals away.

When we finally arrived at Nahá, we camped near the lake. There was mud everywhere. I remember that Chan K'in Viejo kept telling me, "Don't fall!" And so, what was the first thing I did? I fell face first in the mud! Trudi picked me up and took me to the lake to wash me off. She was laughing, and I was shaking with shame and embarrassment.

That was the first time I met Chan K'in Viejo. He spoke softly and kindly to me. I knew right away that he was a very special man. He seemed like a governor or a president. I was impressed that he had so many wives and so many children. Trudi had told me that the Lacandon men had several wives living in the same house. She even made jokes about all the mothers-in-law. But I didn't believe her until I actually saw it with my own eyes.

Chan K'in's wife, Koh, was there with him. She was so young then. There were many families, but I don't remember much about them. The children I met on that first trip are old now.

Later Trudi said, "Chan K'in. This is my daughter." Chan K'in looked surprised, so Trudi explained, "Not from here," pointing to her stomach, "but from here, from the heart." And Chan K'in understood right away.

The trip home left an impression on me too. We returned by a different route, through Monte Líbano and then a place called El Real. We spent the night there, and Trudi taught me to swim in the Santa Cruz River. That trip seemed so short. I didn't want it to end. I loved it so! That was my first visit to the jungle and I will never forget it. It was like a beautiful dream.

When Trudi and Frans were still alive, life was wonderful here in Na Bolom. They loved each other very much, even though Trudi was ill-tempered at times. But we got along well. She liked to work early in the morning, and I always went along with her to learn. She taught me to cook, and I made my first meal after living in Na Bolom for two years. I went around with a notebook to write down recipes. Since Trudi just threw in the ingredients without measuring, I would take a cup and measure the quantities when her back was turned. If I asked her anything, she would just yell at me, because she hated when I asked questions. She was always yelling, and so, to stay out of trouble, I would just watch and not ask questions.

One morning she said to me, "I'm going to take some people horseback riding, and while we're gone, you have to prepare our meal—spinach, ground beef, and rice. Cook the rice with carrots and some chicken stock and chop the onions and herbs. There's cream and cheese in the kitchen. You know how, just look at your recipes. Have everything ready in an hour. And make a salad too. Disinfect the lettuce and tomatoes. Oh, and make an apple pie!"

So I went to pick the apples and made the pie first. It came out perfect. But I hid it. And each dish I prepared I hid from sight inside the oven. Then I saw Trudi riding home at full gallop.

"Beti! Beti!" she screamed. I hid behind the door. Why did I do that? Can you imagine?

Trudi looked for me everywhere. "Where did that damn child go?" She knocked on Don Pancho's door and hollered, "For Christ's sake! She didn't do anything I told her to do." Boy, was she mad! Don Pancho came looking for me, so I came out of hiding and pulled on his pants leg.

"Here she is," he said.

Trudi screamed, "Why did you do this to me?" and began to beat on the tabletop. Of course, I began to cry but managed to say, "The food is ready."

"What? Where is it? I don't see anything!"

Then I opened the oven door and there was everything, even the salad. Four guests came to eat at Na Bolom that day, and they congratulated me on the meal. The next day they asked me what I would be serving for dinner. And that's how I became a cook. After a couple of years, I did everything myself and soon lost my fear of the kitchen.

Dinner was always served at seven o'clock sharp. If people arrived late—whether they were paying guests or Trudi's best friends—they weren't allowed to eat. Nor would she let friends or guests leave food on their plates. "There are people dying of hunger. Finish that! Why take so much if you're not going to eat it? If you didn't like it, then why did you put it on your plate?"

After dinner, which usually ended at twenty to eight, they moved to the library. While the guests sat around the fire, Trudi did her exercises. She would lie down on a big animal skin and twist and turn while she talked with her guests. Later she would fill a washtub from the faucet out in the garden. She would bathe herself first. Then it would be my turn to wash, in the same water. After I went to bed, Trudi and Don Pancho stayed up, reading. Trudi would read her book and knit at the same time. I still have a pair of socks she knitted for me.

Once Don Pancho's brother came to visit. He was such a nice man. Every day we would go to the market together. And if they gave me money to buy food, I would spend it on flowers. Sometimes I would buy nothing but flowers. Doña Trudi would scold me, "Today, no flowers! We can't eat flowers! Food!"

Chan K'in Viejo came to visit us many times. He came on the bus or hitched a ride with friends who were coming back from the jungle. Trudi and Chan K'in were very close. They had a wonderful friendship.

All of my memories, both good and bad, are here in Na Bolom. This is my home. Trudi was tough, but she could also be tender. If she weren't, nobody would have put up with her. It's just that she had no patience. She wanted everything done fast and done well.

Trudi often went to the jungle. When Don Pancho stayed home, we had lots of fun. He would say, "Take Trudi to the airport, and on the way back, stop and buy me a bottle." The only taxi driver in town, Don Emetrio, would bring me home in his taxi, and Don Pancho would say, "Okay, now you can go out with your friends whenever you want." Then he would shut himself in his office until Trudi came home. He would quit drinking a day or two before she returned. Then he would bathe and get dressed, and I would cut his hair. He liked that. For me, it was lots of fun because he would tease me and we would laugh a lot.

Don Pancho was very sweet and had great patience with people. When he worked, Trudi would start a scandal in the kitchen. But when she finally locked herself in her room to write, everything would calm down. There were times when we had very little money. Trudi would have to sell her photographs. I never had much interest in that, even though Don Pancho taught me to print in the darkroom. What a shame, isn't it? If I had talked more with him, we would have discussed such wonderful things. I was so shy back then, and when I think of what I missed, it makes me sad.

When I grew up, the time came for going to parties and having fun. My first boyfriend was a construction worker from Ojo de Agua. How I liked that boy! He was dark, tall, and strong. I really liked dark-skinned men who were big and strong, not skinny. And he was just like that. In those days the boy would first talk to the girl to see if she wanted to be his girlfriend. When he asked me, I said, "Oh, yes! I would love to!" You were allowed to kiss, nothing else. Not like today. And so a year or two would pass like that until it came time to marry.

As I told you, Doña Trudi treated me like a baby and spoiled me so. She said, "I see you talking with that boy a lot."

"Oh, yes," I replied. "But he never told me he was my boyfriend. I just like to talk to him." Trudi tried to make me understand that I was going to suffer. So I told her, "Well, the other day he did ask me if I wanted to marry him."

"Well," said Trudi, "he's your boyfriend, then."

"Oh, but we were just talking."

"Then why is he offering to marry you?"

"Don't worry, I'm not going to marry him," I assured her. But, yes, he was my boyfriend for a while and I liked him a lot.

Once I had another proposal of marriage. After that first wonderful trip to the jungle, I went with Trudi again. The camp where she stayed was near the lake, and Antonio came to visit us with his canoe filled with bananas. He hung around but never spoke to me. I loved his hair, which was long and curly. That's what I most liked about him, his beautiful hair. He was so handsome, but he was always a little afraid of me.

One day Trudi called us over and we walked to the edge of the lake. "Let's talk for a while," she said to us. Antonio squatted down and pulled at his tunic, as he always does. Then Trudi said to me, "He wants to marry you. He likes you a lot. Isn't that right, Antonio?" He uttered a simple "Yes." He touched my hair, my braids, and put his hand on my head.

I pulled away and said, "But I don't want to marry him, Doña Trudi."

Trudi became furious with me and screamed in English, "Shut up!"

After that, Antonio came every day, because he was in love with me. But I didn't even want to see him. Later he said, "Marry me. Don't go away. I have a cornfield and a house." But I said, "I'll come back another day."

"Big mistake!" Trudi told me later. "If you told him you'd come back, it's because you agreed to marry him. You shouldn't play games with him. You should either tell him yes or tell him no."

The next time we returned to Nahá, Antonio already had a wife. But even then he would stare at me. And sometimes he still says, "I remember how you used to come and play the guitar. You had such pretty hair."

But, no matter. Such is life. Later, when I married and had so many problems with my husband, I regretted not marrying Antonio. Even if he had filled me with children, I would have been happier with him. Don't you think so?

I met my husband at a dance. I loved to dance, every day! I used to escape out the window of Na Bolom so I could go to parties. You know, I used to have a German friend whose father had a plantation near Tapachula, and another friend who's the owner of San Nicolás Ranch. They came by one night with an engineer from the north of Mexico and we all went to a party. I met my husband when he asked me to dance. There was another boy I liked, a Nicaraguan boy named Oscar, who was teaching me to dance the way they do in his country. And I confused the two because they looked so much alike.

After the party this boy came to see me every day. Soon he became my boyfriend, and three months later we were married. It all happened so fast. Doña Trudi didn't approve at all, and she told me, "He's just going to break your heart. You'll see."

And that's exactly what happened in the end, but I married him anyway.

In truth, my husband was very . . . how do you say? . . . macho. He wouldn't let me go out or even wear pants. He told me that the man wore the pants in the family. After my daughter was born, I was forced to stay inside the house. For me it was horrible to be stuck inside, and I tried to run away. He stole my daughter and made me go back to him. It was terrible!

But I was so happy with my daughter, so happy. And with all the others too. I love all my children, even though we've had our problems. I don't think I've been such a bad mother.

I've been very lucky to have lived here in Na Bolom. I've met people from all over the world. In 1991 Trudi and I went to Sweden to receive Trudi's prize for her ecological work. The king of Sweden sent a chauffeured limousine to pick us up. They took us on tours of the museums, and we went riding on the canals in the king's boat, which had the symbol of his crown on the prow. The captain was so tall and handsome! But the most exciting thing of all was to dine at the king's palace. Uuuyy! My mouth fell open just to see those walls made of jade and gold. There was a harp of pure gold too. There were huge tables covered with beautiful silverware. I said to myself, "How are we going to eat with all this metal!" The knives and forks were lined up from here to there, and so many glasses all in a row! The waiters were dressed in hats with enormous feathers on each side. Their uniforms looked as if they came out of a fairy tale. When the guests entered the dining room, the waiters bowed to each one.

Do you know that man from the Middle East? The one with that checkered rag on his head. Yasir Arafat? Yes, Yasir Arafat! Well, he was sitting on one side of me and Trudi on the other. He talked to me, but in English, because he spoke very little Spanish. I would watch out of the corner of my eye to see which silverware he would use. They gave me a big glass of wine, and what wine!

Trudi was angry with me and hissed, "Don't get a big head. You're only here because of me. And why are you talking to that stupid, ugly, old man anyway?" At least she remembered to speak to me in Spanish!

I answered her, "I'm paying attention to you, Trudi. I'm not trying to ignore you, but this man is talking to me. What can I do?"

They had given each of us a basket of chocolates. Yasir Arafat asked me, "Do you have any children? Carry these chocolates home to them. You can take them on the airplane with you." So, with his basket, Trudi's, and mine, I had three baskets of chocolates.

Mr. Arafat was such a nice man. He looked after me. When we were served another white wine, he warned, "This wine is stronger than tequila. It will burn your throat." I tasted it, but it wasn't that strong. I didn't drink all of it anyway. Better that I didn't!

After dinner they moved us to another salon to listen to a concert. But what a salon! And I got to know every bathroom in the palace because every few minutes Trudi had to go! One of the bathrooms had a huge seashell overflowing with flowers.

Later that night, when Doña Trudi was called up to receive her medal, she didn't want to take it. I whispered in her ear, "It's yours. Take it."

The king spoke to her in French. Really! He said, "It's for you, Madame." But Trudi screamed at him, "What do you know, stupid! Give it to me!" Then she tried to pull it from his hands and the medal fell to the floor. The king very politely picked it up and handed it to her.

After that, I thought, "This is the last time I go anywhere with her!"

When I think about my future, well, I try not to think about it. Just one day at a time. What will happen to my house? There have been so many changes, and changes scare me. What will happen to my children? They're grown up now, but I still worry about them. I have five grandchildren and would like to see them all with good careers and my sons and daughters with their own houses. It's a lot to ask, don't you think?

I feel happy that I've been able to work until now and that I've paid my way. How awful it would be to live in this house and not contribute in some way. If I had the money, I would love to travel. I would love to get a job as a guide, taking people to the jungle. That way I wouldn't be so tied down here.

I'm seventy years old, and God only knows, it's a lot to ask to live to eighty or ninety. At that age one doesn't live too well. I would be afraid to live alone, without my children or friends. I know that some day death will come to me and I will have to receive it. We just have to accept it as a part of life. But all in all, I've had a wonderful time. I've been truly happy. Yes, it's been a beautiful life!

Juana Koh

Juana Koh

Juana Koh is my name. I'm pretty old, I think. José Güero was my father and Koh María, my mother. Koh María, the wife of Chan K'in Viejo, is my sister. She came before me. I only had twelve brothers and sisters. That's not very many. Only twelve. I was born in Monte Líbano, then moved to Nahá with my husband, Domingo. I was around twelve years old when I married Domingo and went to live with him and his other wife. I was the second.

I never had children. None. Domingo died many years ago when he was still a young man. He died of dysentery, the same as his other wife.

I never got married again. I couldn't have children. The man says, "Children are good. If there are no children, I don't want to get married."

Domingo loved me. Even though I didn't have children, he never hit me. He had two wives, and he didn't hit either of us. After Domingo died, I didn't want to live with his other wife, not anymore.

Now I live with Juan Mendez, my brother. We've been living together for many years. Juan has attacks of epilepsy. The attacks are bad, but it doesn't scare me. I just put a cloth in his mouth so he doesn't bite his tongue.

When my father died, my brother was very little. Now only my brother is left. My father's dead. My first mother—my father's first wife—died too. My real mother, Koh María, lives in Lacanjá. Her hair is white, and she's very, very old. I don't see her anymore because Lacanjá is far away. I don't have the money for the trip.

Everything has changed here in the jungle. Our clothes are not the same. We used to wear the *hach nok* and *hach pik*, the tunic and skirt made of bark cloth. Now we dress in prints and white cotton. That Trudi Blom was my best friend. She used to bring me clothes.

I used to make dolls and incense burners out of clay. My husband would go to Ocosingo to sell them. He walked all the way there and back and slept on the jungle floor at night. He carried the things I made on his back. But once he fell and everything broke.

My husband knew everything about the gods. He drank lots of *balché*. That *balché* is very tasty. My brother, Juan, likes it too. My brother knows how to do the ceremonies but not how to build the god house. No one makes the ceremonies anymore. Just Antonio. His temple is very pretty.

There used to be many animals. Not anymore. There were wild boar, pheasant, deer, and monkeys. Very tasty, the spider monkey. We ate the howler monkey too. But I most like the meat from the wild boar. I used to eat lots of wild boar, because there were so many of them around. *Tepezcuintle* too. But not anymore. Now there are too many people. There are not as many animals because too many people live in the jungle now.

My husband and I used to go out in the jungle all the time to look for howler monkeys, to look for boar. He hunted with nothing but his bow and arrows, because he didn't have a rifle. He would kill the howler monkey very fast, with just his arrows.

And snakes! There were lots of snakes. And they were FAT! I was very afraid of them. My husband always killed them. I was bitten three different times. Once I was in the jungle cutting wood with a machete when a snake bit me on the hand. It was a small fer-de-lance. My arm swelled up to my shoulder. Lots of blood came out of my mouth. I was very sick and stayed in bed for three months. There was no medicine in the jungle. There was no clinic. When someone got sick, the family would carry the sick person on their backs, or in a hammock, all the way to El Capulín, ten kilometers away. I didn't die because I took herbs. But I can't find those herbs anymore.

The jaguars would come and eat everything. They ate my chickens and my dogs. And one time a jaguar came into my house. The house didn't have walls, just a roof. That jaguar came in one side and went out the other. He was big! But he didn't attack us because my husband killed him. We ate that jaguar and sold his pelt.

We ate all the animals my husband killed. We ate everything, even the skin.

I like deer skin a lot. I cooked it, and it tasted very good. Just like pork rinds. I would scrape off the hairs with a machete or put the deer in the fire to burn off the hair. I did the same thing with the monkeys. Monkeys have lots of fat. I'd take it out of the pot and have five liters of monkey fat. We ate it, and it was delicious. Monkey—very tasty!

We used all parts of the animals. We'd use the pheasant feathers and the parrot feathers for arrows. And I'd wear the toucan feathers in my hair. But there are no more feathers because we don't kill the birds anymore.

We used to make money selling our tobacco. With that, we bought *panela*, salt, and oil. The tobacco doesn't grow anymore. I used to like to raise my little pigs, but there are no pigs in Nahá anymore.

I still have my cornfield. I've already cleared and burned it. The corn is already growing, and the birds are eating it. I plant beans, sweet potatoes, and squash. There are grapes, bananas, *chicozapote*, and *mamey*.

I've never been to Palenque. I've never been to San Cristóbal. I did go once to Ocosingo, but, oh, a long time ago. I've never really been out of the jungle. My husband didn't want to go out. He didn't like San Cristóbal or Ocosingo. We just liked the jungle. Always the jungle.

Merle Greene Robertson

Merle Greene Robertson

I've always loved the outdoors. As a child I was a bit of a tomboy and played outside all the time. I was born in Miles City, a little cattle crossing in the middle of Montana. But I actually grew up in Great Falls, on the Missouri River. Every weekend I went hiking along the river or in the mountains.

I had just one brother, who was two years younger than me, and I was always putting him up to doing all kinds of crazy things. My brother and I each had a horse, and unbeknownst to our mother, we would ride bareback across the river to a neighbor's ranch. We pretended we were cowboys, and we'd chase their buffalo, until one day the owners of the ranch heard about it. Then my mom heard about it. And then we heard about it! So we were grounded from the horses for a while. I tell you, we used to get into more trouble on those horses!

I also spent a lot of time in the Olympic Peninsula of Washington State. The rainforests there were just like those down in Mexico and Guatemala. We'd hike or ride in on horseback and camp on the edge of the lakes.

Later I ran a camp for children. We had twenty-four horses and a dozen canoes. I began counseling at the camp when I was in college. Eventually I leased the camp and ran it myself. I had studied anthropology under the famous North American anthropologist Erna Günter. She had a place just a fifteen-minute canoe ride from our camp, and we'd paddle over there for a visit.

Around 1959 I decided to go up to Alaska. The Al-Can Highway had just been built, and I was going to take my two children with me. So I cased out every place where we could find medical attention and where we could buy food and supplies. I bought a new station wagon, fitted it out with a stove, and put a rack on top for the canoe—the whole works. But my family had a fit. "You're going all the way up to Alaska? That's absolutely crazy!" So I said, "Well then, I'll just go in the other direction." If they wouldn't let me go to

Alaska, then I'd just drive to Mexico instead! Of course, I'd never been to Mexico. The fact that I couldn't speak a word of Spanish didn't seem to bother me or my family at all.

So off we went to Zacatecas. It was such fun. And eventually we ended up in San Miguel de Allende. I had always been interested in art, so the children and I enrolled in art school. We spent the whole summer down there. And that was the beginning of everything.

Later I went back to school in San Miguel while my children were off at camp. That summer a friend of mine and I decided to go to Tikal to visit the Maya ruins. First we flew into Guatemala City. We were just planning on staying away from school for the weekend, but we both packed a suitcase full of good clothes. We didn't know what we thought we were going to do with all those clothes, but I remember we each carried a good pair of patent leather pumps.

We got to Tikal stashed between cases and cases of Chivas Regal whiskey that the pilot was dumping off in the jungle. This was not exactly legitimate, you know. The liquor came from Belize, and he was smuggling it in. Somebody was probably going to make a lot of money!

The minute we landed at Tikal, my friend saw a snake, turned around, and got right back on the plane. Did not even go to look at the ruins! Well, that old snake didn't bother me any! So I grabbed my suitcase and off I went to see Tikal. I was enamored immediately. School could be attended to later. I stayed in the jungle all that summer.

Some archaeologists from the University of Pennsylvania were the only ones at the site. They were making new discoveries every day and needed an artist to help record their findings. So I stayed to work with them. I had my painting equipment with me and was doing sketches of the sculptures and hieroglyphs. One day one of the archaeologists was going into Guatemala City and I said, "Bring back a couple of bedsheets. I'll see if I can do some rubbings."

They had just uncovered Altar V, and it was gorgeous. So I tied a sheet around it and dabbed my oil paints over the bas-relief. I reproduced an image of that whole monument. Now you can hardly see the relief because the altar sat in the sun and rain for years before they finally put it in the museum.

At first I just did pen-and-ink drawings of the monuments, carvings, and glyphs, but later I brought down rice paper and did rubbings too. I worked at Tikal with the University of Pennsylvania for three summers.

There were so many animals in the jungle. Once I saw a beautiful black panther walking down from the main plaza. I remember a monkey that figured out how to unlatch the door to our lab, and he dumped out all our vials of photographic chemicals. That was a big disaster!

I loved the jungle. I used to wander off alone, and it never even entered my head to be scared. There were no clear trails between the temple sites like there are today. Sometimes I'd be hiking down a narrow path and I'd come to a fork. "Which way do I go?" I'd ask myself. I'd draw a picture in my sketchpad of each place the trail branched off so that when I was coming back I could see which fork I was supposed to take. I went all over Tikal that way and I never once got lost.

One day Alfred Kidder of the Carnegie Institution said to me, "Merle, why don't you go up and down the Usumacinta River and do rubbings of all the Maya sites." At the time it seemed like nothing.

"Oh yes, sure!" I told him. "I'll go up and down the rivers. It's no big deal."

So I did it. And when I finished with Guatemala I went to Mexico and did the same thing.

That's when I first came to Palenque. I fell in love with the ruins the minute I arrived. I flew in from Villahermosa on a little plane that seemed to be held together with scotch tape and safety pins. Back then, the airport in Villahermosa was a tiny building with a little white picket fence out front to keep people away from the propeller. I was with a German girl who was supposedly going to Palenque too. When the plane came along, she said to me, "You're going on THAT thing?"

"Well, yes," I answered. "How else are we going to get there?"

"Well, I'M not going on that thing!" she cried. And she didn't go.

In Palenque the plane landed in a field by the railroad station. Someone obviously heard the plane coming and came to pick me up in a jeep. The road to the ruins was nothing but a mud rut. It had been a terribly wet rainy season and the whole area in front of the Palace was flooded. A Chol Indian came along and carried me on his back, wading in water up to his chest. I had been given permission to camp out in the Temple of the Sun. None of the ruins had been cleared yet. The fact that I would be sleeping up there by myself didn't bother me one bit. I thought it would be great.

When I started working, I lived at the campsite with Robert Rands and a helper. We were the only people at the ruins. Tourists hadn't started visiting yet. One day the archaeologists went off to the Tulijá Valley to do some ceramic testing. I was there all by myself. I had a lantern but couldn't leave it on for long because the battery wouldn't last. That night I noticed in the lamplight that there was something that looked like a snake draped over the doorway. But I knew it wasn't. I knew it was the electric wire that went from the generator. So I crawled into my cot and went to sleep. In the morning, when I went to get my breakfast of bananas, I saw that the wire was really a *nauyaca*. YIKES! It was HUGE! I had slept with that snake the whole night. At first I thought, "Well, I'll get on a stool and take a shovel and whack at it." But then I realized that he would probably fall down on top of me. So I went to the door, with one eye on the snake and the other eye looking out for Augustine, the elderly man who had been a guard at Palenque forever. He lived across the river, so I began yelling for him. But it was a Sunday and nobody came. Finally, after about an hour, Augustine came ambling up and I told him there was a *nauyaca* inside. He just looked at me like, "This gringa doesn't know what she's talking about." Well, when he went in—uh-oh! He didn't say a word, just went out and came back with a forked stick. He put it around the snake's neck, then calmly pulled out his machete and killed him.

A number of years later, my husband, Bob, and I kept coming back to Palenque often. I just loved it. I thought, "This is it! We've just got to be here!" Soon afterwards, around 1969, we started building our house.

One night at the house, a group of friends were sitting around on the porch telling snake stories. So, of course, I told this story. My friend Linda Schele said nothing. Did not even open her mouth. The next day we were out on the porch again having a beer when Linda came tearing in the door.

"It's true! It's true!"

"What's true?" we all asked.

"Merle's story about the *nauyaca*! I went out to ask Augustine if it was true. And it is!"

Another time I was going to Tikal to do a rubbing for Harvard University. The weather was hot, hot, hot! I went in with two Chol Indians and my student, Don Hart. The going was rough because there was no trail. Suddenly I saw a snake, and I leaped over it while yelling at the top of my lungs, "NAUYACA!" Don was right behind me and slowly began translating this unfamiliar Spanish word. "Na-u-ya-ca … let's see, let's see, let's … Oh! FER-DE-LANCE!"

When Don got back to school, he told everybody that they should kick my husband, who was dean of the school, out of his position as track coach because when I jumped over that snake I could leap faster and higher than anybody on his track team.

Over the years everybody I know has gotten malaria except for me. Everybody! Once in Belize I got dysentery from drinking coffee made with contaminated water. The next day I was really, really sick and stayed sick for a long time. But other than that, I've never had a problem. And I've been in the jungles for more than forty years. I guess I'm just tough.

I don't get sick, but what I do is break bones. I've broken my head, both elbows, my ankle, and my knee. I've broken just about everything there is to be broken. The only thing that bothers me is my right knee where I tore the ligaments while working at Chichén Itza two years ago. I had to have it operated on, but it never really recovered. Every once in a while it goes out when I'm walking on uneven ground, and that's when I have to use a cane.

I've never fallen off a temple, and I've climbed over all the temples in Palenque, clear up to the roof combs. That's the only way I could do my drawings. My assistant, Chencho, would raise a ladder and I'd climb up. Then he would hold me so I could lean back to see what I was drawing. I'd lean back in his arms, knowing that he wouldn't let me fall. And, of course, he never did.

I have no fear. I never refused to do anything just because I thought it might be dangerous. Which, thinking about it now, kind of startles me. Once we were working at a site where I was recording monuments. The site was at the top of a mountain, and it was a difficult job climbing up to it. I had six students with me. When we got up to the site we saw that looters had been in the process of stealing the monuments. While some of my students were helping me with the rubbings, others were collecting all the evidence they could find, like empty packs of cigarettes and oil cans where the robbers greased the saws they used to cut away the carvings.

When I finished doing the rubbings, we went back to our jeep, dead tired. It was so hot. I was just kicking off my boots to get in the jeep when along came six men with sawed-off machine guns aimed right at us. I wasn't too worried because they had police badges on. I had a letter that gave me police protection in the jungle. So I thought that as soon as they saw my letter they would know who we were. When I reached for the letter in my hip pocket, my Belizean assistant whispered under his breath, "No! Don't move, and don't talk to them!" But soon I got tired of having a gun pointed at my stomach, pulled out the letter anyway, and handed it to them. They read it and let us go. Later one of my students said, "You know, those were fake badges."

Of course I went to the police station as soon as we got back to town. The police asked, "What did the men's hands look like?"

"Well, they looked like anybody's hands," I answered.

"Oh, then they were city guys who were in the jungle trying to make some money by looting archaeological sites." They must have thought that we were stealing the pieces that they were planning to steal! That's when I realized that if we ever met again, the robbers would surely recognize me because I was the only blond-haired woman in the jungle!

I've spent my whole life recording the art of Mesoamerica for the benefit of future scholars. I've done about four thousand rubbings of carvings, glyphs, and monuments in sites all over Mexico and Guatemala. The rubbings are all at Tulane University, in the Merle Greene Robertson Rare Book Collection.

I've done rubbings in all the archaeological sites in Chiapas. I've worked in Palenque, Toniná, Yaxchilán, Bonampak, all up and down the Usumacinta River. I've recorded everything at Palenque, doing both drawings and rubbings. I've made plans of every inch of the ruins and studied every speck of paint on every structure. I've made measurements that don't even show up in any book because there are too many of them to record.

I worked for weeks on the sarcophagus in Pakal's tomb at Palenque. I did rubbings first and later took photographs. The rubbings were done in sections, of course, because the rice paper measured just three feet by six feet. It took a lot of paper. I did those rubbings in oils instead of sumi ink. I was locked in each day so the tourists wouldn't come in, and I had to wait until someone let me out. Once I was locked in the tomb with no light. So I tore off a piece of the rice paper and wrote a long letter to my mother telling her what it was like living down there in the tomb.

Unfortunately, tourists aren't able to see the sides of the sarcophagus because there's so little space around it. In 1965 I took a Hasselblad camera, measured the distance between the sarcophagus and the wall, and photographed the sides. It was difficult because I couldn't get my head in there to see what I was doing. I photographed the carvings on the walls of the tomb and those under the stairs. I had a hard time crawling under there to photograph the rest of those figures. Everything was covered with something like seven-minute frosting, crisp on the outside, but if you punched it, your finger would go right in. It's a wonder the carvings are still there. Anyway, all of those photos are published in my four-volume book titled *Sculpture of Palenque*.

Something that always puzzled me was how the ancient Maya made the paint for their murals, especially the gorgeous Maya blue. That special color was apparently made in different ways. We know that cochineal used to be found around Palenque. Mixed with agapurtite, it will turn into that particular blue color.

Once we found a cave near Palenque that was completely covered with that same blue. It looked exactly like the Maya blue they used in their murals. We decided to go in and get some, but there were a million and one bees living inside the cave. So we borrowed our friends' bee helmets and gloves and brought out two buckets full of the blue, even though the bees were after us. We had kept the engine running, with the jeep heading downhill, so we could jump in fast and make our getaway. Luckily, we weren't stung too badly. But as soon as we ground up our stash, it turned a pale, pale blue. It wasn't at all the color it had been inside the cave.

Chencho and I used to go back into the Tulijá Valley, hunting for ways the Maya could have made their paint. At some sites they added lime to the blue to make it turn greenish. So, for two years I was slaking lime. We stored the slaked lime in a big tub in the lower part of our house, and after two years we were about ready to test it. One day Chencho ran out of things to do, so I guess he decided to clean out this tub. He dumped out all the slaked lime that had taken me two years to make! Ohhhhhhh! What could I say to him? Nothing. He didn't do it on purpose. He was just trying to be helpful.

Once we cut a path into a site near Palenque and found a reddish yellow ochre that was exactly the same color the ancient Maya had used. There was so much of it that we could have painted the whole state of Chiapas with what we found. We were chopping that color out of the mountainside and getting bucketfuls of it. We wanted to test it out. But we never did get the lime to test the color with!

When I was at the art school in San Miguel de Allende I took fresco-painting classes with one of Mexico's foremost muralists. Those classes helped me a lot when I got to Palenque. I'm convinced that the ancient Maya painted their murals like the early Greeks did, which is a modified fresco different from the frescoes done in the Renaissance. I think the Maya kept their murals wet for up to three weeks so that they could do large areas at a time. So they must have done them during the rainy season, not the dry season. I'm sure this is the way they did it.

For two years I had grants from National Geographic, which helped me to record the deterioration of the monuments caused by acid rain and dry deposition. I had thought that vandalism would be the number one culprit for the destruction of the monuments. But that was down at the bottom of the list. Dry deposition was at the top. As rain falls, it contains acid that can come from as far away as the oil fields in Veracruz. If the force of the rain falls directly on the carvings, the acid pretty much washes off. But if the rain drips down slowly, the acid keeps accumulating, and it turns everything black. It got so bad at Palenque, and I complained about it for so long, that finally I sent a whole book full of photos to the governor of Chiapas to see if he could do something about it. The National Institute of Archaeology and History sent restorers in from Mexico City to clean everything. They were in the process of cleaning when the Chichonal volcano blew up. After that, the restorers left.

The volcano spewed tons of ash that fell directly on the ruins. The temples looked gorgeous, but the ash was very destructive. We didn't have rain for weeks, and when it finally came, the water cleaned everything like a high-powered scouring powder. The carvings on the eastern court figures, which are on a slope, were literally washed off.

There was so much ash in town that the residents had to shovel it off their roofs into the middle of the streets. The piles were six feet deep. Little children would take big dives into the ash, and it would kick up like talcum powder. A doctor friend of mine said, "Boy, these kids are really going to have respiratory problems one day!" Trucks were brought in to take the piles of ash away, but they just dumped it on the outskirts of town. And when the wind blew, the ash came right back into town!

It was impossible to breathe with all the ash in the atmosphere. Many people left town, even the mayor. The ash was so corrosive that it ate the cuffs right off my pants and made the soles of my shoes fall off. I didn't want to abandon my work. But before long I had to leave Palenque for a while because the ash was beginning to affect my ears and lungs.

One of the best things about my more than four decades in Chiapas is the friends I've made. I've known just about everybody in the world of archaeology. Linda Schele was my best friend. She came down to Palenque and fell in love with it just like I did. We hit it off right away.

Another good friend was Trudi Blom. We got along great. The first time I met Trudi was at Sayaxché. I arrived after dark, and in the middle of the night I heard someone screaming and swearing out on the porch where the bathroom was. You weren't supposed to lock the bathroom door from the inside. But that person had locked it, and she couldn't get out. Trudi was the one who was cussing up and down inside that bathroom. That was my introduction to the famous Trudi Blom.

One time Linda and I and some others from Palenque went to the ruins of Chinkultik, and afterwards we stayed over at Trudi's place in San Cristóbal. It was terribly cold. Linda was so sick the whole time we were at Chinkultik that she could hardly climb up the main pyramid. Later we all ate at Na Bolom. Trudi was sitting at the dinner table with her two great big dogs on either side of her. I was sitting next to Trudi, and Linda was next to me. When we finished eating, someone came to take our plates away. Trudi looked right at Linda and shouted, "I was taught when I was a child to eat everything on my plate!" Linda began sinking down farther and farther in her chair, which wasn't very easy because Linda was quite a large woman. I spoke up and said, "Trudi, this is the first time Linda has eaten anything on this whole trip. She's been sick." "Oh?" says Trudi. "What's the matter with Linda?" After that it was a different story. Then she just wanted to look after Linda. We had a puppy with us that I had bought for five pesos in Comitán. Trudi wanted to look after him too. She insisted that the puppy eat big slices of beef right off a roast she brought from the kitchen. I thought, "If anybody comes to visit Trudi, they should always bring a puppy along."

Trudi used to come to all the Round Tables we had in Palenque. She would go to hear every single speaker, which is more than you can say for most people.

Our Palenque Round Tables started when a group of us were sitting on my back porch one evening, having a beer. We got to thinking, "Wouldn't it be nice if we got people together who are interested in Palenque and have them come down here and share what we know or don't know about the Maya." When I went back to teach school in September, I was coming through the front door and the phone was ringing. I hadn't even taken off my jacket yet. It was a friend saying, "Let's get together this Christmas." I said, "Okay." Everyone made his own arrangements, came down, and met at my house. We sat on chairs, beds, floors. We kept a pot of coffee on the stove. People brought their children, and we decorated a Christmas tree. We had such a wonderful time that we did it again the next year. After that, people wanted to stay home for Christmas, so we started having the meetings in June. We began with thirty-five people. At the last two Round Tables we had three hundred fifty and then four hundred fifty people. That's a lot! They came from thirteen countries and from all the major universities in the United States and Mexico. The residents of Palenque were really excited about it. They spent the whole year preparing dances and such. But after twenty years I got tired of doing it. It was too much work! So I turned it over to Mexico. But the next year it was a real flop! The second time Mexico did it, they asked me to help organize it and it was a real success.

Right now I'm working in Palenque on Temple XX. And I've been working at Chichén Viejo too. I swore I wouldn't write any more articles, but I've ended up doing that also. I've written over one hundred books and articles. I did my undergraduate work at the University of Washington, received my Master of Fine Arts from the University of Guanajuato's Institute Allende and an honorary doctorate from Tulane University.

Tulane recently sent out the director of Latin American Studies, and for three days we went over everything. They also sent the person in charge of all my rubbings, and he spent a week here, all day, every day. We inventoried everything and packed up twenty-eight huge boxes. I have four cases made out of black Bakelite, which is incredibly strong. They've been in canoes up and down rivers. They've been over mountains on horseback and muleback and on planes. That's how I carried my rubbings around for forty years, and they're still in good shape. They all went to Tulane University. Plus, I've sent them my thirty-six field books. Anybody who wants to know anything about the Maya site of Palenque just has to go to Tulane. All of my life's work is there in one spot.

A long time ago a street in Palenque was named after me, and there's a federal school in Chiapas named for me too. In 1994 the Mexican government gave me the Aztec Eagle Award, which is the highest award given to a non-national. It was presented to me for recording and preserving much of the art of Mexico. It was quite an honor, and I was excited to receive it.

We're learning new things every day about the ancient Maya. New sites are being discovered all the time. I remember when I first became involved in the Maya I thought, "This is much more interesting than Egyptology, because the world already knows everything about that. All you have to do is read books about it." Of course, now I know that's not exactly true. But that was my opinion back then. In Egyptology, you just read about all the wonderful discoveries, but with the Maya, you actually go out and do it!

I am and always have been adventuresome, that's for sure. I'm curious too. And I've always been creative, even when I was just running a camp for children. I was always figuring out new things to do.

You know, it's interesting how just one small thing can change your whole life. If I hadn't gone to Tikal so many years ago, I would probably be teaching art someplace. But I always wanted to see things and go places to find out what was going on there. Chiapas was one place I wanted to see. The difference was that when I first saw the ruins at Palenque that was it. From then on there was nothing else for me but the Maya.

María Patishtán Likanchitón

María Patishtán Likanchitón

I never knew my father. I always lived with my mother and my four brothers and sisters, three from my father and the fourth from another man. We were all born in the community of Zetelton, in the municipality of San Juan Chamula. I am sixty years old now, and I just have one sister left, but we don't talk much anymore.

Our life was hard. My mother was very poor. We had three tortillas to eat every day, nothing else. We ate in the morning and then nothing again until nighttime. There was no food in my childhood. No chicken, no meat, no sacks of anything. There was nothing to cook . . . nothing, nothing.

My mother was always weaving. She knew how to weave like the Chamulas, and also in the Tenejapa style. She made cushions and blankets. After my father died, that's what she did. Weaving, always weaving. And I learned to weave from her. First I learned to comb the wool. Then I learned to make the thread. And at last I learned to weave. My mother taught me everything. She also taught me how to plant corn, potatoes, squash, and peas. My mother is dead now. My poor mother died twelve years ago.

I was fifteen years old when I married Salvador. I was really in love with him. What I most liked about him was that he had beans and corn. He planted my corn down in hot country. He worked hard, and he didn't drink that much. Just once or twice a year. Of course, he hit me, but since he drank just a few times a year, he only hit me a few times a year! Salvador was responsible. We only had one child, because we were only married for two years. And then he died. Suddenly he got sick to his stomach. His belly got very full. He threw up and shit and died three days later.

I was very sad when my poor husband died. Yes, very sad. My son was just one year old. I was seventeen. But no, no, no, I never got married again. I was thinking inside my head and I thought, "Better all alone. I like it better alone."

If there's a man around, he tells you how to do everything, tells you if this is right or wrong. Then he drinks a lot and there's no food. So I was always thinking to myself, "I work on this thing and the other and I don't make much money, but at least I have enough to buy beans and corn and meat."

But when my husband dies, I'm not doing very well. I don't have any beans or corn. No, I don't have anything. I don't go out, and I'm very hungry. And I'm thinking inside my head, "What happened? How can I work? I don't have a house. I don't have a piece of land. I don't have money. I don't have anything." So I say my prayers. I carry my candle and my incense and I go inside the church. And I ask God, "What's going on, God? Where's my money? Where's my house? My piece of land? My food? I don't have anything, God. What's going to happen to me?" That's how I prayed. "Dear God, take care of me. I don't have anything."

And I was thinking like that for a little while and soon came a lady, Marta Turok. She was an anthropologist working for the National Indigenous Institute. So I began to work with Marta. I made nice weavings, nice shawls. I made *chucs*, the wool tunics the Chamula men wear. We carried them to Mexico City. They were nice. I sold the *chucs* for three hundred pesos apiece. That was a lot of money! And that's how I started to work. I made many trips to Mexico City. I would weave there too. I sold my things at the Indigenous Institute and at the Museum of Popular Arts. I worked with Marta for two years. Then I worked with Chip Morris and Pedro Meza at Sna Jolobil. I worked with everybody.

Suddenly, since I was doing well, the people from my community thought I was an Evangelist. I never thought about converting to Evangelism, never. I was never going to change my customs, never in my life. But all the people came together to talk to me. And they talked and talked and finally said, "Come on! Let's throw her in jail!" They wanted to put me in jail for being an Evangelist. Those fucking people don't know a thing! They're envious and they're liars. But I wasn't afraid. I said, "Okay. Put me in jail!"

So they took me to the jail in Chamula. But I didn't end up with very much jail, just five or ten minutes' worth. They let me out because I accepted the position of *mayordoma*. "If you really aren't an Evangelist, then accept the position of *mayordoma*," they said. That was bad. The position means a lot of work, and it costs a lot of money. And there's a lot of liquor. "Well, okay," I said. But I was happy to be a *mayordoma*. I was with Christ Our Lord.

I had to sell liquor so they'd see that I wasn't an Evangelist. I had to sell *posh* to pay for all the soft drinks, all the liquor, everything I needed for all the ceremonies and festivals. But there were lots of parties and lots of drinking, and I did very well. I sold lots of *posh*. Lots! I sold it all day long and all night too.

And then I started thinking inside my head, "There's my sister, Petrona, at the house, and she makes *chucs* and shawls and blouses and bags and dolls." I was having problems with Sna Jolobil, and I didn't want to work with them anymore. I wanted to organize my own group of artisans. I wanted to sell for the women and make some money to buy my piece of land and my house. I thought to myself, "Half the money will go to the women and the other half to me."

So I went with my son to Mexico City to sell our crafts. But the first time we went alone to Mexico City I was very sad. Since I didn't go with Marta, I didn't have a place to sell my merchandise. There were so many streets! I didn't know how to read. I didn't know where the arts and crafts market was. I didn't have money to buy food. But finally I sold some little bags and then some bigger ones. I sold each thing, little by little. Saturdays and Sundays I would go with my son to sell in the streets, and it was good. Soon I learned where I could sell my things in Mexico City.

I used to go to Mexico City three or four times a year. Now I only go once or twice a year. I travel with my grandson, Marcelino. Last time we met a professor from Michoacán who invited us to a lot of craft fairs. That's how we went to Toluca and to Guadalajara. At the end of this month we're going to Leon, Guanajuato, Monterrey, and to San Luis Potosí.

Once I went to the United States. I didn't enjoy the trip. No, I didn't like it at all. We went to Phoenix. I liked the place, but I didn't like the people I traveled with. I don't know how to read and write, and I think the people I went with cheated me. We stayed in Phoenix for a week, and I wove and sold my things in the Phoenix museum. I met a lot of people, and they told me that my work was good. But I didn't get along with the people I went with. They didn't pay me what they should have.

Then we went to visit the Navajo Indians. What I didn't like at all was that the Navajos eat sheep. Those Navajos eat nothing but sheep! I don't like to eat sheep. It's just not right. Roasted chicken is all right. Rabbit too. You can eat cows, but just a little. Other animals, yes. But sheep, no! We Chamulas don't eat our sheep.

So I didn't like the food. The burritos were okay. I ate just once a day. Now I would go back to the United States to visit, but I'd go by myself. I definitely would not go back to visit the Navajos who eat sheep.

When I returned to Mexico I was mad, and the people I traveled with were mad at me. "Fucking María," they said.

Now I live in Chamula. My son left his family and has another wife. But my four grandchildren and their mother live with me. I sell my weavings, and when tourists come, I sell well. Lately not many people pass by. Some tour guides don't like me and won't bring their tourists to my house. But there's enough food for me and my grandchildren. There's enough for everybody.

My life has been many weavings and many travels. I've gone to Puebla, Tapachula, Cozumel, Tabasco, and to Mérida. I went three times to Oaxaca, and I went to Durango. I travel a lot. It's wonderful to travel, really, really, wonderful.

But I never thought inside my head about leaving Chamula to live someplace else. No. Chamula is my place. It's a very good place. The Fiesta of San Juan and all the parties here are so much fun! And I would never leave my church. My church is beautiful. It does my heart good just to look at it.

It was a great honor to hold the position of *mayordoma* three times. I finished my religious responsibilities last Christmas. Now I'm in bad shape because I borrowed so much money. I asked for many, many loans. Now I can't pay them back. I owe more than one hundred and fifty thousand pesos, because I served for three years, and each year, more loans. Every twenty days during those three years I had to change the flowers in the church, make a party, and pay for the musicians, liquor, soft drinks, more liquor, and food. Every twenty days for three years is a big expense. Spending and spending. Now I'm trying to sell whatever I can of my crafts in order to pay off my loans.

I would like to live for many more years. I still have a lot of energy. And I have a plan for my life. When I pay off all the money I owe I'm going to start a new life. I have an idea in my head to buy a car, a Volkswagen van, so my grandson and I can travel in it—slowly, nicely. We'll go wherever we want in our car. It's good to have a car so that I can carry all my weavings, to Mexico City or wherever. I'll go with my grandson. He just has to say, "Let's go!"

Carlota Zepeda Gallegos

Carlota Zepeda Gallegos

I was very young when General Venustiano Carranza and his revolutionary troops came to Chiapas to put an end to the plantations. They invaded the ranches and threw their owners into jail. My father had inherited two ranches, the Golonchán and the San Fernando, near Pantelhó. He was among those who were jailed.

The Golonchán ranch is where Sub-Commander Marcos and the Zapatistas are now. Very well done, I say! They did well to take over my father's ranch. If I ever have a chance to meet Marcos, I would shake his hand and congratulate him.

Well, when Carranza took over the plantations, the owners had to pay a high bail in order to be released from jail. My father had to sell almost all that he had to get together his bail money. At that time my mother was pregnant with her fourth child. When our family suddenly lost the ranches and all our money, my mother became desperate and left us. She abandoned us and went back to live with her parents. What a difficult situation! I was her second child, born in 1915, and when she left, I was four years old. I remember that my mother was a good-looking woman and my father loved her very much. But she became confused and abandoned my father, Rosa, Fernando, and me.

So my brother, sister, and I grew up with my father's sister in San Cristóbal. We called her Mama. At our house we also had an Indian maid from Bachajón who did all the chores. She was a good worker and was very faithful to us. Those two women took care of us and brought us up after my mother went away.

Aunt Elvira specialized in making candied fruits in syrup, a tradition in San Cristóbal. My aunt Rebecca made crepe paper flowers, straw houses, and straw churches, which were used in Christmas nativity scenes. I learned to make things out of straw, and we sold them during the Christmas season in order to earn a little money. Another aunt, Manuelita, always told us stories and jokes and taught us to recite. She was paralyzed for life one cold day in December because she took a hot bath after doing the cooking. That proves that it's very dangerous to bathe with hot water after working in the kitchen, especially when it's cold outside.

We all worked hard just to be able to eat. We washed clothes, ironed, and prepared food. My father taught us to write even before we went to school. My grandmother, who had a lot of influence in town, managed to get us into a private school. I enjoyed it there, but after I finished primary school I couldn't continue. I didn't have time to study because I had to work.

I met my future husband, Erasto Urbina García, at a political gathering given by the Institutional Revolutionary Party, or PRI. I was a member of the PRI along with many other women. In those days it wasn't so uncommon for women to be in politics.

Erasto was a dark-skinned man from a humble family. Back then, there were people in San Cristóbal who were very racist. And since Erasto was dark and poor, many people treated him badly.

But Erasto was very studious and curious about life. He owned many books and read constantly. He owned a hardware store, but he aspired to something more. He dedicated his life to defending Indians and laborers. And to that end he studied hard and mixed with many people in politics. He ascended in the party, but when he ran for mayor of San Cristóbal, the Coletos rose up in arms against him.

My father was a friend of his, and he told me, "Certain people want to kill Erasto. He's an irreproachable man, hardworking, humble, but very intelligent. Come, my daughter, let's pray for him." And so I prayed.

When the Coletos went after Erasto, he hid behind one of the trees that grew in front of the cathedral. But his enemies managed to shoot off two fingers on his left hand. Miraculously, Erasto's friends and followers were there, and they defended their leader. Years later, when Erasto was finally elected mayor, he asked permission to cut down all the trees in front of the cathedral.

He never wanted to see them again because they reminded him of that terrible incident. As mayor, he cleaned the trash from the streets and made San Cristóbal safe for its inhabitants.

After Erasto was almost killed, a group of us girls who worked together at the PRI office went to visit him. He thanked us profusely for that visit. Erasto was nineteen years older than me. He had been married and had a son, Javier. After his wife died and he was left alone, all the girls flirted with him.

But he fell in love with me, and after a while he approached me, "Look, Carlotita, you know I'm a widower. I want to start my life over and I'm thinking of remarrying."

"Oh, how nice, Don Erasto," I replied. "Please invite me to your wedding."

"No," he said. "I'm talking about you and me."

"Oh, thank you very much," I answered.

"Carlotita, I want to marry you," he insisted.

"Oh, but Don Erasto, this is extremely serious. You don't even know me. We don't even know if we'll get along."

"Of course we would," he answered. "I've known you since you were little. I have a son, but he won't be living with us."

"That's the least of it," I said. "I know how to treat people, and I'm sure that your son won't be angry with me. My father is your friend, Don Erasto. It's better that you talk with him about these things."

I was in love with him. Of course I was. I liked him because he was precise and loving and never talked nonsense or was vulgar.

My father later told me, "Look, my daughter, Erasto talked to me about his intentions. You know that he is a hardworking, intelligent man. He hasn't made much money because he is so honest. But he already has a seven-year-old son who might not agree with your marriage."

"The boy will be fine," I said.

But my father repeated, "Erasto is a great man. Think about it, daughter. You're the one who will be living with him."

We were married on December 24, 1938. After our honeymoon in Tuxtla Gutiérrez, we returned to live in the *Mexicanos* neighborhood of San Cristóbal.

Little Javier came to live with us. He had been living with his aunt and resented having to live with me. He behaved rudely toward me because he was mad at his papa. He would demand a weekly allowance and then throw the money back at me. But I never paid any attention to that. He was jealous, and with good reason. Later he became friends with all of his half brothers and showed me much respect. He turned out to be a good man and still calls me on the telephone.

I had seven children with Erasto. All of their births were easy because I have a strong character. No one but the midwife helped me give birth. Erasto would call the doctor, and the doctor would come and drink coffee and chat. Yes, during the birth, Erasto would prepare the doctor with talk and coffee. Where are you going to find a man like that!

All my children are still alive, except for my oldest son, Erasto. How I regret his death. Sometimes, even though I don't want to, I still cry for him. He was good and honest and a hard worker, just like his father. He had many girlfriends but finally fell in love with one of those girls who thought she was something special. Those two youngsters were very much in love, but when they decided to get married, her family sent her off to the United States. After she left, my son began to drink and later became addicted. He decided to give in to the alcohol. Eventually he married a fabulous woman, and they had a daughter together. But he could never give up the drinking and finally died of cirrhosis of the liver.

I had a wonderful marriage with Erasto. He never yelled at me and never told me what to do. But I understood how he was and never went anywhere without letting him know where I was going. I never went out of the house just to pass the time. No. I went shopping at the market, took the children places, and went to mass, that's all. He gave me freedom, but I went out only with his permission. He would say, "Get dressed up, Blondie, so that you can go visit your aunt."

Our relationship was beautiful, a mutual understanding without words. I've never known of another marriage like ours. He was a marvelous man. I never had any problem of any kind with Erasto because I always did what he wanted. So we never fought, nor were there ever any cross words between us. When he was worried about his work, I would make him special teas to settle his stomach.

We used to hire a woman to do the family laundry, but Erasto didn't want her to wash the children's clothes. I had to wash them myself. If Erasto had been a dishonest politician and had robbed the people, then we would have had more things. But he was an honest man, so we never had a washing machine. Erasto always told me, "No, I don't want a washing machine. It's just going to break down and won't be worth anything. It's better that the woman washes our clothes and you wash the children's." After so many years of washing clothes with harsh detergents, just look at the spots I have on my arms!

As I told you before, Erasto dedicated his life to defending the workingmen and the poor Indians. He fought for their right to receive a fair salary, something that was not very common in those days. Erasto was a revolutionary, but a high-class one. People were naturally drawn to him. Even foreigners like Doña Trudi Blom valued his friendship and sought his advice. That's why his friend, President Lázaro Cárdenas, liked him so much. The president used to come to our house often. We gave banquets for him. What an elegant man he was!

Erasto's birthday parties were always something special. All of San Cristóbal came to congratulate him. They brought marimba music and a band of musicians and huge piles of tamales. We would set out enormous tables and cover them with long cloths. The house would be full of people because Erasto was so well loved. They recognized his dedication to his ideals. The only people who didn't love him were those who were against the Indians.

Large groups of Indians used to come to our house to eat and spend the night. They came to talk to Erasto, who spoke Tzotzil and Tzeltal perfectly. I got along well with most of the Indians who came to our house but not with all of them. I couldn't speak their language.

"How good that you like to talk to the Indians," I told him.

He would say, "Of course I talk to them. My enemies might put someone in my house who wants to kill me. And the one who loses out will be me! I have to talk to my Indian friends to make sure there are no traitors among them."

I never got involved in politics myself. I was a wife and housekeeper. But I supported my husband's ideals with all my heart. I always agreed with whatever he did, and to this day I think that he was correct in all of his decisions.

His ideals were very similar to those of the Zapatistas. But Erasto was a politician of great quality. The PRI was more revolutionary back then. The times were different. The difference between Sub-Commander Marcos and Erasto wasn't in their attitudes or their ideals. The difference is that Marcos is young, innocent, and inexperienced. Erasto was an established politician who never used arms. He never resorted to violence.

Poor Marcos! If he had just had Erasto's experience he would have done better. He wouldn't have used violence. No! He would have tried to find a solution through purely political means. He would have found a better way. But throughout history it's been the same: many people want to take advantage of the poor workers and the Indians.

Erasto passed away in 1959. His death still makes me sad. After he was gone and there was no more money in our bank account, I had to sell the house to pay off his debts. Erasto had bought my grandparents' house because he loved it so much. All my children were born there, and that was where he died. I wish I had never had to sell it, but there was no alternative. I rented another house and lived in peace there, without owing a cent to anyone.

After I was widowed, our friend Dr. Manuel Velasco Suárez, the ex-governor of Chiapas, took my children and me to Mexico City. I worked for five years in Tepexpan, teaching handcrafts to the doctor's recuperating patients. Twenty-four women worked for me. But one day my five-year-old daughter, Eréndira, went across the street to visit a friend and somehow got lost. Eventually my son, Erasto, found her, but after that scare, I didn't want to live in the big city anymore. We moved back to San Cristóbal, and I got a job as the librarian at the technical school. I worked there for many years and then later in the public library. If I hadn't come back to San Cristóbal, I would have retired in Mexico City and all my children would have finished their studies. Sometimes I wonder if I should have stayed.

None of my children followed in their father's footsteps, even though they admired his accomplishments. God has rewarded my children and me for all that Erasto did for the Indians. We've always been healthy and happy. Yes, the Lord has watched over us all because of Erasto's goodness. That's the way I see it.

I'm happy with my life, and I'm in good health. But I can't remember how long I've been in this home for old people here in Tuxtla. Sometimes I forget things. I came here because I needed to break away a little from the family, so that when I die they won't miss me so much. They need to get used to me not being around. Since I came to the home, my children have found their own paths in life.

But I get bored because there's nothing for me to do here. I would like to make myself useful, but I suffer so much from the heat of Tuxtla. I think I've been here long enough. I want to go back home to San Cristóbal now.

Luvia Amalia Burguete Sánchez

Luvia Amalia Burguete Sánchez

My father was a big landowner who had several ranches, one of which was La Quinta del Carmen, just outside San Cristóbal. My great-grandfather, Ponciano Solorzano, bought La Quinta from the church bishops to use as a country house. Great-grandfather was the first liberal in Chiapas, and they murdered him because of it.

I have only wonderful memories of my father, who was a sweet, handsome, and good-hearted man. My mother was quite beautiful and very intelligent. Before she married, she ran her own business. After marriage, she looked after my father and helped him with the bookkeeping for the ranches. I was born in San Cristóbal on December 8, 1908.

My father loved to eat sweets, and during the fruit season, his aunt used to make candied fruits for him. Since I liked sweets too, my great-aunt taught me to make my own candies. I'd put them out on the dining table, and when my father came home, all tired from work, he would see the candy and eat a few pieces. Later he would tell me that he owed me for the sweets he had eaten. He paid me because he loved me. So that's how, at a young age, I became a businesswoman. From the money my father paid me I bought the sugar and all the ingredients that I needed, reinvesting the capital.

I also did business with my sisters. I would measure their dolls and then make little dresses for them with scraps of cloth. Once the clothes were made, I would dress the dolls and say to my sisters, "Look how good they look! If you want them, it will cost you this much." Since my sisters didn't like to sew, they would have to buy from me. I saved most of what my father and sisters paid me, so I always had money. Of all the daughters, I was the rich one.

I spent my savings each year at the festival of Corpus Christi. Back then, everybody dressed up in their new clothes to go to the Pontifical Mass, which was very solemn. After mass, all the churchgoers went to buy candy at the Zebadúa Arcade, where the vendors sold their delicious sweets. People bought huge quantities of candy to exchange with their friends, *compadres*, and family members. That day in San Cristóbal was "sweetheart day." The night before, the boys would serenade their girlfriends, and the next day they would give them candy along with a big bouquet of flowers.

One Corpus Christi Day, when I was eight years old, I took my savings and bought a lot of that fuschia-colored candy, which is so popular here, and I ate every bit of it. That night I told my father that I wanted to sleep with him in his bed. My mother was against it because I tossed and turned and kept my father awake. Eventually I got my way. Around midnight I was so restless that he tried to rouse me, but I wouldn't respond. My father woke my mother so that she could check on me, but she couldn't wake me up either. Mother became worried and called the doctor right away.

The doctor lived across the street. He came immediately and saw that I was seriously ill. He applied a poultice using half a kilo of ground mustard seed. The treatment consisted of placing a folded sheet on top of me, then sprinkling the ground mustard seed on top of the sheet, and wrapping me inside. Over the sheet they poured boiling water, making sure they didn't scald me. They let the poultice sit until it cooled, then repeated the process.

The doctor stayed with me all night, and when I opened my eyes at daybreak, he said that I would survive. For a year after that, I stuttered when I spoke. My mother thought I'd never speak again, but eventually I recovered completely.

When I was ten years old, there was an epidemic of the Spanish influenza. The illness started as a bad cold and then affected the organs—liver, kidneys, and pancreas—until the person became very weak. So many people died that they couldn't bury them all. The municipal government dug mass graves and buried everyone there. Indians passed through the streets in ox-drawn wagons picking up the bodies that had been left out on the sidewalks. The entire town locked themselves in their houses so they wouldn't become infected. No one went out into the streets except when it was necessary to buy food. Even then, only the servants were sent out.

My father had a niece who went to the bakery to buy bread. She would come by our house to leave half of what she bought, and that's how we had something to eat. If she found out that a butcher was going to slaughter a cow, she would go at four or five o'clock in the morning to buy meat for us.

One day a relative who was worried about our family came by to see how we were doing. He was terrified of catching the Spanish flu. After he left our house he stopped at a cantina to have a whiskey and then bought a bottle of liquor to drink on his way home. With that he got drunk, of course, and passed out in the street. When the wagoneers saw him lying there, they thought he was just another dead person, so they threw him in the back of the cart with the rest of the bodies. The clacking noise of the wagon wheels passing over the cobblestones woke him up from his drunken stupor. When he realized that he was lying in a pile of dead bodies he jumped down from the wagon, terrified, and ran all the way home in a panic. But he was already infected and died soon afterwards, along with so many others.

Many doctors were infected and died during the epidemic. I was always very curious about what was happening outside, but my family wouldn't let me go out of the house. One day I was looking through the little hole in the front door and saw some men hauling a coffin from the house across the street. I went to tell my sisters that someone had just died. It was my parents' dear friend, Dr. Juan Velasco Dubois, the one who had saved my life.

When I was twelve years old, my father died from problems with his gall bladder. We were all so sad. To this day, it makes me cry. My father's death was just too hard for me. When he passed away, the happiest time of my life ended with him.

After my father died, my family life changed completely. My mother married another man and had five more children with him. I always got along very well with my two sisters, but we did not get along with our mother's new husband. We were always angry with him, so we went to live with my grandmother. We were very mischievous, or at least I was. I loved to play outside and to climb trees. My grandmother was very strict with us. She loved us very much, but she set firm rules.

My sister Célia had a special talent for playing the piano. My father was very proud of her, and from the time Célia was four years old he hired special teachers for her. At that age her fingers weren't long enough to reach all the keys, so they tied sticks to her fingers so she could play. When she was older, her dream was to attend the National Conservatory of Music in Mexico City. At last our uncle offered to take her to the school. There was room in his car for another person, so he said, "Let Amalia go too!"

Altogether it took us eight days to get to Mexico City because the driver didn't know the way. When we finally arrived we went to live at the guesthouse of Doña Carmen Camacho, who was a good friend of my mother and my grandmother. Doña Carmen took me to visit an uncle who was a judge on the Supreme Court. Since I knew how to type a little, he gave me a job as a typist in the courthouse. A year later my sister Flor joined us. Then my mother separated from her second husband, and she and my grandmother came to live with us too.

Mexico City was a beautiful place back then. I always enjoyed going out, but I had to beg my grandmother for permission each time, until she finally gave in. There were many people from San Cristóbal living in the city, and on Sunday afternoons we organized dances and other social events. My mother and grandmother always gave us permission to attend those reunions. And people often gathered at our house because my sister played the piano.

Célia graduated from the conservatory and became very successful, giving concerts on Radio XEW from Sunday to Thursday at six o'clock in the afternoon. In San Cristóbal, big speakers were set up in the municipal building, by order of the mayor, so that local people could listen to her play. My sister always wanted me to accompany her to the Radio XEW studio. She would say to me, "If you don't go with me, then when you have a boyfriend, I won't go with you either!" But I wasn't very popular.

My sister Flor had a boyfriend in San Cristóbal. They would have been very happy together if they had married. But his family intervened because my mother had just married her third husband. Back then, divorces were frowned upon. Meanwhile, the brother of Flor's boyfriend was killed by a jealous rival. It was a big scandal.

Later my mother and sisters moved to Cuernavaca because they said it was easier to find work there. But I was making good money in Mexico City and finally had a boyfriend whom I loved very much. My sister tried to convince me to come to Cuernavaca because she wanted me to meet "a very handsome little doctor named Bernardino who dances very well." I loved to dance, so I was indecisive. At last they convinced me, and I went to Cuernavaca to live. There I had the bad luck of meeting the famous little doctor. Immediately he began to flirt with me. I didn't pay any attention to him because I was in love with my boyfriend, who came to visit me often. One Saturday my boyfriend was supposed to come but never arrived because his father fell ill. So, believing that he had stood me up, I went to a dance where I saw the famous little doctor. Right away he started flirting with me. He told me that if we didn't get married that very day he would go away and never bother me again. Since I was disappointed that my boyfriend hadn't come to see me, I told Bernardino that, yes, I would marry him, thinking it would be impossible to arrange a wedding so late in the afternoon.

What a surprise I had when Bernardino arrived at nine o'clock that night with a judge and witnesses, everything quickly arranged because his godfather was the mayor of Cuernavaca. I couldn't believe what was happening, because in those days it was very difficult to obtain marriage papers. I hid in the kitchen and told my sisters that I didn't want to marry the doctor. "Then why did you tell him you would?" they scolded. "Why did you let him arrange all the papers and spend so much money?"

So I got married, even though I wasn't in love with Bernardino. I was still very much in love with my sweetheart. My intention was to run away with him as soon as possible. But I lost track of him and didn't hear from him again until a year after I married. My sister Flor brought me a letter from my boyfriend explaining why he had not come to Cuernavaca that weekend. But it was too late.

I didn't live with my husband at first. I lived with my mother until she decided to move to Iguala, Guerrero. When she was packing up, she told me I had no choice, I would have to go and live with my husband. So, Bernardino and I went to live near my mother in Iguala.

Bernardino was an affectionate man, but he was unfaithful. And there was no one in the whole world more jealous. He'd lock me up in the house so that no one could see me, and he wouldn't let me go out alone. When we went out together, he would make me walk with my eyes cast downward so that I couldn't speak to anyone. And if by misfortune I would turn around to look at someone, he would get mad and start an argument. Meanwhile, he would flirt with every woman who passed by. Even after I had my first daughter, Scherezada María Antonieta, my husband kept cheating on me. People told me so. I was very unhappy with the life I was living with my husband.

When I had my second daughter, Yol-yztma, my grandmother and a cousin came to visit my new daughter and me. They told me they wanted to see the famous Casino de la Selva before they returned to Chiapas. Because my baby daughter was sick, I couldn't go with them, but Bernardino offered to take them dancing. When they arrived at the casino, Bernardino sat my grandmother and cousin down at a table and ordered a bottle of liquor. Then he went off to dance with a girl and soon disappeared, leaving my relatives sitting alone all night. Since Bernardino came home at seven the next morning, I assumed they all had a great time. When my grandmother and cousin came by the house that afternoon, they didn't say anything about the night before. When I asked them how they had liked the casino, they changed the subject. After we ate we said good-bye, since they were returning to Mexico City and Chiapas the following morning. To my surprise, my cousin came to the house the next day saying that my grandmother wanted to know if I'd like to go back to Chiapas with them. She explained that Bernardino had gone off with a girl and had left them sitting alone in the casino. At first they didn't want to say anything but later decided to tell me so that I could think about whether I wanted to continue living with him. I already knew about his infidelity because a neighbor had told me that my husband was seeing other women around the corner from my house. Then and there I chose to leave Bernardino and return to Chiapas with my family. A few minutes later I regretted it and told my cousin I would stay. I couldn't make up my mind. I kept packing my bags, then unpacking them.

"Hurry up," my cousin told me. "If Bernardino finds you like this, he'll get mad." At one o'clock, just before Bernardino came home, I finally decided to go. I didn't take anything with me, not even my clothes.

That night Bernardino came to Mexico City to convince me to go back with him. He insisted, but by then I had made up my mind to return to Chiapas with my grandmother.

Back in Chiapas, we lived in Tuxtla Gutiérrez, where the weather was hot. Because of the awful heat, my daughters came down with malaria and were sick for almost a year. I was so afraid they were going to die. Bernardino wrote, trying to convince me to return to him. "Don't be stupid, come back," he wrote. Once, in desperation, I thought, "If one of my girls dies because of my stubborn decision to stay here, I won't be able to stand it." When I told my mother I was thinking of going back to Bernardino, she got mad. "Why don't you think things through? Don't think that this man is going to change. A man never changes. You're just going to go and come back pregnant with another child."

But I did go back to my husband. And, dear God, there on the corner by the house, women were still waiting for him. He loved me, but he wouldn't give up his other women. And, of course, I immediately became pregnant. My mother wrote to me asking if my husband had changed and if he was treating me well. But I lied to her, saying that things were fine. Then I had my third daughter, whom we named Berenice. She was six months old before my mother knew I had another child. I was afraid to tell her.

One day she wrote a letter asking if I was being careful about getting pregnant. That's when I told her that I couldn't stand living with Bernardino anymore and asked her to come to get me.

My mother did come for me, and I went back to live with her in San Cristóbal. Bernardino kept writing me. I still have a stack of letters that I never answered. He offered to buy things for the girls, and he told me he missed me. But he never helped us in any way. Ten years later he came to Chiapas with his sister to convince me to go back with him, but I didn't go because I knew what would be waiting for me there.

When I think about my marriage I feel nothing but disappointment. The biggest mistake of my life was marrying Bernardino. I gave up so much by marrying a man I didn't love. After we were married, he didn't even want to dance with me anymore! I was never tempted to remarry, and I've never missed having a man by my side. I was just happy to be free!

When Bernardino died, I didn't want to go to the funeral. But my daughter María Antonieta went. She later told me there were about twenty women crying over his casket. She told me, "Oh, Mother, how right you were to leave him and come back to Chiapas to live."

Here in San Cristóbal I had to support my daughters. My mother proposed that I take charge of our La Quinta ranch. Only a part of the ranch was left after the new land reform laws. La Quinta was one of the first sawmills in the state. My mother stayed in San Cristóbal to sell the wood. My sister Flor and I took turns going out for a week at a time to manage things. When it was my turn, my three daughters and I walked there or rode out on horseback. Apart from my children, I loved the ranch more than anything in my life. There I felt free. I spent my happiest moments there. We had fabulous parties. I lived in harmony with God's grandeur.

One night the ranch was attacked by a group of Indians led by the infamous Erasto Urbina. They wanted me to leave so they could take possession of the land. So Don Erasto sent men to burn down my house. At daybreak my daughters and I were asleep. I woke up when I heard shouts. I remember thinking, "For sure one of the bulls got stuck in the river." But suddenly I understood what the Indians were shouting: "Fire!"

I jumped out of bed and ran to the door of the living room. The house was in flames. First they burned down the barn where the crops for the whole year were stored. It was right next to the living room. When I saw the barn caving in, I screamed, "My daughters are sleeping in the bedrooms!" I grabbed the youngest and pulled the other two out of harm's way. I was in my nightgown, but I put on my pistol. I handed my daughters to the Indians, who saved them. Then one group of Indians started drawing water from the river to put out the blaze while the rest began cutting the rafters so the fire wouldn't spread to the other house.

I ran back inside to see what I could salvage from the fire. When I saw the flames licking my father's portrait, I called to one of the Indians and told him, "Let's take down my father's picture." By then the flames had completely engulfed the door. I escaped out a window and the Indian passed the photograph down to me.

A minute later the roof fell in, and everyone thought I was trapped inside. When they saw me come out alive, the men shouted with joy. No one was killed, but the house was burned to the ground.

The next day I sent a boy to tell my mother and sister what had happened. They immediately rented a car and came to drive us back to San Cristóbal. I told them to take my daughters. I would stay.

I endured a lot of harassment from the Indians living nearby. At night they would jump around the house with their machetes to try to scare me. But because I showed them that I wasn't afraid, they calmed down and began to speak to me, and later we became friends. The house was rebuilt, but we never lived in it again.

Once I met Don Erasto Urbina in person. It was his birthday, and all of San Cristóbal was there. One of my cousins said to me, "Amalia, let's go to Don Erasto's party to congratulate him and to see what faces he makes when he sees you!" I was very afraid, but we went anyway. When he saw me he exclaimed, "Just look! My little enemy has come to visit my humble home." And from that moment on, he treated me very well. Because I was very nervous, the liquor they served me that night had no effect at all. I stayed at the party until late and enjoyed myself immensely. After that, Don Erasto never bothered me again.

The hardest thing I have had to endure in my life has been the death of my two daughters. My eldest daughter, María Antonieta, died fourteen years ago. It seems like yesterday. The youngest, Berenice, died of leukemia at the age of eight. What a horrible illness! I went to so many doctors, but in those days they didn't know very much about that disease. It began with an intestinal fever, and later my daughter turned yellow. So much blood poured from her little nose. At the end, the doctors wanted to give her an injection of snake venom, which supposedly often gave good results. So I said, "Give it to her." But it didn't help at all. I think she knew she was going to die. The day after the injection she was lying in bed and I told her, "Wake up, I'm going to give you your medicine." And she asked me, "Mommy, what for?" An hour later she died.

After her death, Bernardino wrote me, "Stupid! If you had come back to me, the doctors here would have saved her."

The good thing about having been married is that the Lord gave me three wonderful daughters. Nowadays I enjoy being with my daughter Yol-yztma, my five grandchildren, and eight great-grandchildren. The only thing left for me is to die and to do God's will. Meanwhile, I take pleasure in each remaining day.

Minerva Penagos Gutiérrez

Minerva Penagos Gutiérrez

I'm Minerva Penagos Gutiérrez. I was born on the twenty-first of January in the city of San Cristóbal de las Casas. My mother was born in San Cristóbal. My father was originally from a well-to-do family in Simojovel.

My grandparents had coffee ranches. My father told us that he and his brothers were sent to study in San Cristóbal because it was a city with culture where they would be able to develop intellectually. They used to travel over the mountains by way of Pantelhó, San Andrés, and Chamula, and when they arrived on Sunday evenings, he loved to hear the music playing in town. After my father married my mother, he settled here because the city fascinated him. I imagine that San Cristóbal back then must have been very majestic, very European.

After he graduated from school, my father went to Orizaba, in Veracruz, to finish his studies as an accountant. Then he returned to Simojovel but often came to San Cristóbal for a visit. My grandmother had a house on Crescencio Rosas Street, near the sausage factory. When my father came to visit, he stayed at her house. That is where he met my mother during a family party.

My mother was beautiful in her own way, and my father was a good dancer. At that time my mother was a shopkeeper who had a factory that made clothes for Indians. From that marriage, four children were born, one boy and three girls.

We had a nice childhood even though we had some problems, like all families. Nothing is ever perfect. It was a wonderful time in my life because of the affection, attention, and discipline that my parents gave us. Each time my father returned from his work in Mexico City he would bring us pretty clothes from the nicest shops. We were happy because we had dolls and toys. My sisters and I were very spoiled.

One year we celebrated my birthday on the day of the birth of the Baby Jesus. My mother woke me up early, and later we had cake with our cousins.

My parents loved to give parties for us children but never for themselves.

But one Sunday, when I was four or five years old, my parents went out to attend a baptism. The maid was washing dishes in the kitchen when a pot of boiling water tipped over and fell on top of me. By the time my mother came home from the party, the maid had attended to me, but to this day I still have scars from the burns on my neck and chest. Thank God, I wasn't left with scars on my face.

When kids at school would say mean things about my scars, I would come home from school crying, and my parents would console me. Both my mother and my father taught me that kids can be cruel and that the accident wasn't my fault. My parents helped me get through that horrible experience, and that's why I adored them. When those kids made fun of me, it hurt so much, but at least I had my parents' love. The scars will always be a part of who I am. They have made me how I am today, much more humane.

Of course, my parents fired the maid and gave me preferential treatment. The only thing my father would never let me do was have plastic surgery, so I had to put it out of my mind. But the accident will forever stay in my memory, not so much the burn itself, but how the children made me suffer because of it. Perhaps it's vanity, but now I feel superior to all of those kids who treated me so badly.

My children have even told me, "Look, Mama, if you didn't have your scars, you wouldn't be our mother!" That's why I love them so much. And when my husband and I were courting, he never asked me what had caused the scars. That's why he's the love of my life!

What I most appreciated about my childhood was that my mother and father remained together. All around us were so many broken homes, but we were united, my mother, my father, and the four children. My family made me proud.

Well, there were other children, children outside the marriage, but they were my father's. In spite of the difficulties, my mother was always faithful to him, and in the end my father recognized that.

My relationship with my brother and sisters was like that of all children.

Sometimes we would get mad at one another and fight or poke one another under the table. My father always told us that despite the inconveniences of being girls we should respect our older brother. And then our brother would do certain things.... But why do I even bring that up? My father, in the time he was with us, always told us that we should be like the cogs in a clock. He brought us up to be independent, even though we had to respect our older brother.

What I regret most is that my father didn't live long enough to give me away at my wedding. Of course, my brother took his place. But I never had the pleasure of having my father walk me down the aisle.

I wasn't very popular. No, no, no. I once had a boyfriend, but because of fate or destiny, our relationship didn't work out. But eventually I did find a marvelous husband.

You know, I met my husband in a very nice way. There's a time in each person's life when they are ready to get married. Plus, I had the experience of a frustrated relationship. I had just finished high school and was studying law at night school when I received an anonymous telegram on my birthday.

"Oh! Who could it be? Someone is interested in me! Who has noticed me?" I didn't have any idea who it was. But it filled me with pride. He knew me, but I didn't know him. So when the telegram arrived on my birthday, I said, "Wow! How sweet!"

Those things capture your heart. And when I finally met César, well, truthfully, he knew how to win me over. He knew how to make me happy, how to live a more beautiful life. He pulled me out of the sadness I felt for the loss of that other boy. He knew how to make me fall in love with him.

My parents always told me, "If you don't marry that boy, another one will come along who is much smarter and who will realize how valuable you are." And there's no doubt that my father was right, because that's just what happened. As I said, I fell in love with César because he showed me so much affection, comfort, and attention. They never met, and I don't compare the two, but my husband gave me the same level of respect, protection, and love as my father had. César's loyalty to me was invaluable. And now with all the security in the world I can say that he was never unfaithful to me, because he passed away many years ago and no one has ever come to tell me otherwise.

You know, César gave the impression of being very serious. But when I was with him, he sometimes told me off-color jokes. He also talked to me about the nature of his work as an accountant. There was a lot of communication between us. He was a hard worker but also very sociable and outgoing. What I most loved about my husband, besides his faithfulness, was that he never drank. He drank sometimes, of course, but he was never aggressive. And you know what? He didn't like to dance, but he learned just for me! Oh, yes, I'm a big dancer! I thank God for giving me such a marvelous husband.

When we married, he didn't want me to work, even though I had always worked in sales. But my mother helped me start my own business, which I've managed now for more than thirty years. When my first daughter was born, we opened the store and then we bought this house. So I've always had my business and at the same time looked after my husband and the children.

My children. You know, sometimes people don't understand this, and it's not that I don't love my daughters, because I love both of them very much, but my son was the first, and it's an enormous joy, a gift from God, to give birth to the opposite sex. I love all three of my children equally and always try to treat them the same, just like our parents treated us. But for a woman to give birth to a boy is a wonderful miracle.

I've seen many changes in the world. We knew about world events because my parents taught us to read the newspapers. The death of President Kennedy was very painful for me. He had been my idol.

Then there were the riots of 1968 in Tlaltelolco. Perhaps because of the way we were brought up, with so much discipline, we knew that those young students were heading down the wrong path. And so the massacre didn't affect us as much as those who lost their loved ones. No, what happened to them didn't break my heart. I think they had to be stopped. Those youngsters were very, very passionate about communism. We had seen the overthrow of Batista in Cuba when Castro took over. Back then, when students came to San

Cristóbal, people here would say, "Oh, they're communists! The communists are coming!"

I think one of the biggest changes in San Cristóbal was the arrival of Don Samuel Ruiz. There was a clash between him and our community. I'm glad this new bishop has put things back on the right track.

Because of the religious education my parents gave us, I dedicated myself to raising my children correctly. When they were adolescents, the hippie movement was very strong. We lived through it! Yes, we even heard a little of the music of those times. But those hippies went to the extreme, which is bad. Oh, how those pregnant girls danced during the eclipse! They should have been more careful. And just look how they ended up.

With the type of business I had, selling arts and crafts, we came into contact with many tourists. Many youngsters traveled here during their school vacation. It was a time for them to let off steam and be free. That changed San Cristóbal a lot. After our young people saw that kind of behavior, they broke away from their mothers and ran away from home. Yes, they left their families. How was I going to control my children without them resenting it? That's the art of parenting! Somehow my family survived all of those changes.

In my day we went to school and then came home to help with the work in the house. Children always had their chores. There wasn't this immorality we have today. Now kids just grab their backpacks and leave, without valuing work and chastity. I've seen parents send their kids out into the streets to keep them from getting underfoot. With all this promiscuity, values have been lost.

My parents always talked to us about sex with all the frankness in the world. Not with obscene words—no, no—but saying things like, "Be careful because soon you will develop into a woman." And you know, with all the freedom there is now—well, your first time is your first time. And if you're not careful, you're in trouble.

I notice a big change in young people today. There's so much promiscuity and so much mistrust. Two women can't talk anymore without someone wondering what they're doing. And when you're talking to a male friend, he's only thinking of going to bed with you. How horrible!

On the radio they talk about nothing but sex or homosexuality. What kind of parents those children must have, to be talking about nothing but that. What a lack of love! Because when you have the love of your parents, you may stumble, but you'll never fall.

The affection of my loved ones has made me more humane, closer to God. Even with all the sadness in my life, I feel a deep contentment. It hurts that my husband, César, is no longer with me. But as a mother and as a woman I'm very grateful that my children took care and arrived pure and chaste on their wedding days. They listened to me, and that fills me with satisfaction, because I am a reflection of my parents and my children are a reflection of my marriage. My daughters experienced the joy of giving themselves to their husbands chastely and with dignity. They didn't let us down. I thank God for that and for the determination César and I had in educating our children correctly. God gave me a wonderful husband and family.

What I would most like to do now is get up the courage to travel. I'm a homebody, so going out would be a novelty. I've always been a little afraid of traveling. But in the school of life I have learned that if you give yourself to God and have patience, anything is possible.

Ana María Refugio Pineda Gómez

Ana María Refugio Pineda Gómez

My memory fails me as to the year I was born, but I'm a good bit younger than my sister, Natividad, who is ninety-eight years old. I was born in El Torrente, my grandfather's ranch in the mountains outside San Cristóbal. I moved into San Cristóbal after my mother died, so I've lived here most of my life. I was very sad when my mother passed away. I loved her very much. We used to eat together and sleep in the same bed.

When I was young I used to think about getting married and having a family. I said to myself, "Yes, yes, yes." But when someone would come around, I'd say, "That one is very ugly and that one too poor and that other, too dark." Perhaps they saw me that way too. All my life I was looking for a better man, always someone better. But we can do nothing without the will of God. I'm like I am because God made me this way. He wanted me to be a spiritual mother.

One day a gentleman said to me, "It's too bad you never got married."

But I answered him, "Who do you think has more children, your wife or me?"

"Oh, you shouldn't ruin your reputation like that!" he scolded.

God has given me hundreds of spiritual children. The woman who marries is encircled by family, by husband, children, and in-laws. Then the circle closes around them. But those who decide not to marry and to dedicate themselves to God's service are completely open. Their words have no borders because they have given themselves to God. After having served as a catechist with Bishop Samuel Ruiz for more than forty-three years, I now have an extensive family.

The church never used to teach children about religion. They concentrated on the adults. But when Don Samuel Ruiz came to serve as the bishop of San Cristóbal, he developed a concern for the children. He wanted them to grow up with Christian values.

The faithful came together in a meeting called the Catholic Action. But Don Samuel said, "The Catholic Action is just a chance for men to put on elegant suits and for women to cover their heads with a beautiful mantilla and to show them off at church." No one paid attention to the young ones.

The harvest is big, but those who yield are very few, and so Don Samuel organized more catechists to teach our children. I knew how to pray a little and how to instruct in the Christian doctrine. I have been authorized to give catechism classes here in my house. There is a great need for my work.

In order to construct the most elegant house, the poorest, dirtiest laborer must first dig the ditch so that the foundation can be poured. I am that poor, dirty laborer digging around down in the dirt so that the house won't fall down on top of the residents; so that when it storms, rains, and hails they will still be protected; so that our children have a firm base and won't lose their way; so that they will know that God is the beginning, the end, and the foundation of everything. First one must teach the creation of the human species so that the child learns that we are not animals but children of God, made by the hand of God. God is the way, the light, and the guide.

The doors of Mexico were once closed to other religious sects. But during the presidency of Elías Calles, new sects were allowed to enter our country. The Protestant sects have harmed Mexico a great deal. Now everyone says and does whatever he wants.

Jehovah means "God Our Father" in Hebrew. In Tzeltal Maya the word is "Tatic," and in Tzotzil Maya it is "Totic." The only thing that changes is the language. But without a doubt, the God is the same.

I've worked with Don Samuel Ruiz for many years and know that he is a very good man. The people who have talked badly about him resented him because he treated everyone equally. They thought that a man with money should receive preference over a poor farmer. But Don Samuel said that we are all equal in God's eyes. That's what many people didn't like, and so they began to say that the bishop was advising the Indians to rebel. The situation grew more complicated, and the people became confused. They blamed Don Samuel when, in reality, he didn't know anything about the Zapatista Movement.

The truth is that Don Samuel had nothing to do with the conflict. For years the Indians would come from all over Chiapas to ask for help at the municipal building. Two weeks or a month would go by, and no one in the government would resolve their problems. They would come with their blankets and plastic tarpaulins and sit day and night in the rain. But no one paid any attention to them, and their situation stayed the same. The authorities wouldn't resolve the Indians' problems concerning health, schools, and land. Until one day the Indians got together, found their Marcos, and rose up in arms. They organized their own men and took over the municipal building on January 1, 1994.

That same night I had an invitation to eat dinner with Don Samuel Ruiz, but I had a terrible headache and decided to stay home. But Don Samuel told me exactly what happened that night. He and his guests ate late, because they had been waiting for me to arrive. After the guests left and Don Samuel went to bed, someone knocked on the door of the Episcopal House to advise him that the Zapatista rebels had entered San Cristóbal. He was surprised and saddened by the news. He went to the second floor of his house and opened the window. There was a great multitude of people in the park. The Zapatistas knocked and knocked and even tried to break down his door, but Don Samuel wouldn't open it for them because he didn't want to get involved. Afterwards, many people said that he was one of the organizers of the rebellion, but he didn't even know what was happening.

Now this Marcos, who knows where they found him! Yes, he seemed to be a brave man. And, yes, the Zapatista Movement helped the poor people. Before then, no one paid any attention to the Indians and the poor. No one took them into account. On the contrary, just the word "Indian" annoyed the Ladinos. And so they were forced to rise up in arms because the government didn't meet their demands. But ever since Marcos helped the Indians, they've begun to rebel too much. Now they ask for too much, just too much. I think that the rest of us won't get anything as long as the government is giving everything to the Indians. The Indians keep asking for more, and the more the government gives them, the worse they act. They even have money to buy machine guns. The Indians themselves admit that they are able to be guerrillas because the government has supported them with money. Before the conflict, the Indians weren't armed and everything was much more peaceful.

You see, we won't stay in this life forever. From nothingness a child is born. He develops from a baby into a youngster, then an adolescent, teenager, student, and parent. He moves from maturity into old age and then into senility. After that comes a mound of earth and the grave. From that grave a saint rises into heaven. That is what death is. Death is to be reborn. There is no pain, no sadness, no tears, no suffering, no old age, nothing but pure pleasure.

I know all about death. God has had a place saved for us ever since he first made the heavens and the earth. Our place is waiting for us, and we must fill it some day. Our bodily remains will stay on earth, but we will present our souls to heaven, according to our actions here on earth. I have an abiding hope that the Son of God will receive me when we finally meet in heaven.

Koh Martínez

Koh Martínez

My name is Koh Martínez. I guess I'm about seventy-five years old. I was born in Nahá when everyone lived on the other side of the lake. My mother and father were born there too. I had five sisters and one brother. Well, I had many brothers and sisters, but some of them died. Just six of us lived. At first my father had one wife, but later he married my mother's sister. Then he had two wives.

When I got married I was around nine years old. Yes, I was very young. When I went to live with my husband, Mateo, I was very happy. I already knew how to make tortillas and tamales and everything. I started having children when I was twelve years old. I had ten children, and they all lived, except for one son. My husband had two other wives. I was the one in the middle.

When Mateo and I married, my husband's face was already covered with scars. His mother didn't take good care of him when he was a baby, and he fell from his hammock right into the fire. His face and head were completely burned. But I liked him like that. To me, he was very handsome. And all of my children were born beautiful. That's why I loved him so much. He died just a year ago after living for many, many years.

I never left the jungle very often. I just walked in the forest, went to the cornfield, and worked in the house. My husband would go to sell his bows and arrows in Palenque, Ocosingo, San Cristóbal, and Tenosique. There weren't any roads then, so he went by foot, carrying his bows and arrows on his back. But I always stayed home to take care of the house.

We lived across the lake then. But there was no drinking water on the other side. We had to walk an hour, sometimes at night, just to find it. Here the water is close by, so we're happier.

There were so many animals in the jungle. My husband would go out hunting for howler monkeys and pheasant. We used to eat very well. We planted corn and squash, sweet potatoes and beans. Yes, we ate very well.

I used to be able to work in the cornfield all day, carrying my babies on my back. I always had my babies here at home, all by myself. I would just drink warm *atole de pozol*. The heat from the *atole* would take away the pain. My children made me happy. I'm healthy, so I never had any problems when they were born, none at all.

Every time I was about to give birth, my husband would run out to the god house to pray. And the birth would pass quickly. The gods would help me. The gods have power.

We used to get sick less than we do now. Or maybe it's because I'm getting old. But when I got sick, my husband would chant to the gods so that I would get well. And the gods always listened. The gods knew. I'm still alive because they cured me. Now when someone gets sick, there's just medicine, but it doesn't help.

The men would pray for us whenever we were sick. The men could enter the god house whenever they wanted. Women weren't allowed to pray. Women were never allowed to enter the temple because the gods wouldn't allow it. The women worked in the ceremonial kitchen making *atole* and tamales. We women always listened from the kitchen, but we couldn't go in. Just the men. They are the ones with the power to talk to our gods. But women, no. After the men went to the temple to feed the gods, the women were allowed to drink *balché*. The women would drink apart from the men, always apart, at the end of the ceremony.

My husband prayed a lot to the gods. But when my husband got old and sick, he couldn't pray anymore. He quit going to look for his gods because he couldn't walk to the god house.

His god pots aren't in the temple anymore. Just four months ago my sons took them out to the caves. Only the men are allowed to touch them. Chan K'in Viejo's temple is still there, but my husband's god pots are gone.

Now hardly anyone goes to the temple. Nobody remembers the gods. Just old Antonio keeps going. Before my husband died, he asked our sons, "Who's going to want to take care of our gods?" Not a single one! It made my husband very sad. None of my sons care anything about the gods. They learned another religion. Everything's changed because no one is praying to our gods.

I didn't change my religion. The others, yes, but me, no. I keep going on naturally. Like always. I don't go to the Evangelical church.

Now I work every day cutting firewood and cooking food. I plant my own corn. Along with my corn, I plant beans and chayote. I look for someone to help me, though. My cornfield is in the mountains, about a half hour away. I have to walk from my field carrying the corn on my back. The corn is heavy—really, really heavy. I make my own tortillas and eat them with salt. Sometimes I have chicken or beans or sweet potatoes.

We used to live a little sadly here in the jungle because there weren't many people and we didn't have many things. Now I like it better because there are lots of things. I like clothes and shoes. We used to wear clothes made out of *hach hun*, tree bark. But the fibers itched a lot. Every so often I'd have to go to the river and wet my tunic so it wouldn't be so stiff. When the *chicleros* started working in the jungle, we began to buy cloth from them to make our clothes.

The old people used to wear the *hach u*, necklaces made out of white San Pedro seeds. Nowadays we gather the red seeds to make necklaces for the tourists. But I make my own necklaces out of glass beads. I like all the pretty colors. And I still wear toucan and parrot feathers in my hair.

When there's *majahual*, I make my baskets and my bags. I used to make clay dolls and clay bowls. But I have to search for the clay that won't break easily, so I don't make bowls much anymore. I like my plastic plates better. We used to have only clay pots, but they always fell and broke. Now we have store-bought pots.

But I still don't like to leave the jungle. Out there, there's no place to go to the bathroom. I don't understand Spanish and they don't understand Lacandon Maya, so I can't talk to anyone. I don't like to go to San Cristóbal because I can't ask for my food. I almost faint from hunger. Here in my place I don't have to ask anybody for anything because I know where to go and who to ask for food. If I spoke Spanish I could say, "Could you sell me a little food?" I would starve to death if I didn't live in the jungle.

When I die I'll go to the other world to see Mateo. When my husband went away, when he changed over to the other world, he was happy. He just appeared there, and he was very happy. He became young again.

If I died right now, from natural causes, we would meet each other over there. But if the jungle is destroyed and the world ends, we won't meet again. We'll all go into the darkness. If not, I'll be happy because I'll see my husband again. When my son Bor died, he found his father over there, and they were happy. They're there talking to each other right now. Chan K'in is with them too.

The last time I went to the cemetery I could hear something there. Now I don't go anymore because I'm afraid of what I'll hear. If you go, you'll be afraid too! Those over in the other world cry out to us because they can't see our faces. We won't see each other until we die. And since we're still alive, we can't talk to them. It makes me sad that I can't get close to my dead. But everybody over there in the other world is happy and talking, Mateo, Chan K'in Viejo, and all the family.

Dolores Rovelo Argüelles

Dolores Rovelo Argüelles

I was born in 1931, just after my parents moved from Comitán to San Cristóbal. I can say that my childhood was wonderful because my parents got along very well. There was a great deal of communication in our family. My parents taught us good manners. And they especially taught us to respect everyone. We went to the best schools available.

My father came from a family that customarily sent their sons and daughters away from home to study. And so, after third grade, my parents sent me to the boarding school of the Sisters of St. Teresa in Mexico City. To this day I feel that it was unfair to send me away at such a young age. I was only eleven years old! I didn't know anyone in Mexico City! When I told my parents I didn't want to go, they said they were sending me to boarding school so that I could prepare myself for a better life. During the whole four-day trip—in the car, on the train—I was terrified. I was afraid they were going to leave me all alone in that terrible, faraway place, with no one but strangers.

When we got off the train in Mexico City, I met my aunt and my tutor. To my relief, my aunt was kind to me, and soon I felt comfortable with the Sisters. The nuns were very understanding women and teachers. I had confidence in them. The mother superior was French, and I still remember that her name was Angela. School was hard at first because the subjects were more advanced. But in fifth grade I caught up and began to enjoy classes, especially mathematics.

At the end of sixth grade, I came home for my sister Flor's wedding. I thought I would return to study mathematics with the Sisters, but once I was home my parents decided I should stay so that my brother could go away to school. Again I felt sad. Just when I had the opportunity to study more, they took that chance away from me.

At the Tepeyac School in San Cristóbal, I learned to decorate cakes, make cookies, and do machine embroidery. By the time I graduated, my little sister was away at school and I was left alone with my parents. I felt frustrated that my brothers, sisters, and friends had gone away to study and I couldn't. But I didn't stay frustrated for long. I couldn't leave my parents all alone. What else could I do?

I remember my mother and father with immense affection. They often took us on trips to Mexico City and to the Yucatán. And they always bought us things of good quality. I can say absolutely nothing bad about my mother. I could talk to her like a friend. Even though it hurt not to be able to study, it wasn't a sacrifice to have to stay with my parents. I was very happy and satisfied.

Since I was outgoing, I always had many get-togethers. I used to meet a group of girlfriends every Sunday. We made parties, celebrated our birthdays, and drank coffee together. Or we'd go to an ice-cream parlor, La Vedalia, which was very popular back then. Lots of young people, sweethearts and friends, went to La Vedalia. We would hang out there, talking and telling jokes and listening to music on the jukebox.

Sweethearts! My parents were very strict about boys. My father worked for a while as a dentist. But when my grandfather inherited a ranch on the banks of the Grijalva River, my father had to take care of the ranch. He would come and go, and in between, my uncle looked after us. And this uncle, oh Jesus, he wouldn't let us out the door! Wherever we went, our uncle was there. He was my mother's brother who never had children, so he dedicated himself completely to keeping watch over us. He was so jealous, and, of course, that was inconvenient for us. But sometimes we were able to trick him and escape.

"Where are you going?" he would ask.

"To visit a friend," we would say. Every once in a while I would escape and talk to a boy. But sometimes we would go to a little party. We'd only go for a short while because we were never permitted to be out alone after eight o'clock at night. If we arrived late, we were punished and not allowed to go out again. Sometimes we'd be so excited and happy at a party that we'd arrive home at eight-fifteen or eight-thirty and then have a big scolding waiting for us. The parties were decent ones. We would have a drink or two, nothing more.

And there were many serenades. Usually the boys would get together, supposedly to study, but instead they would tease each other about their girlfriends. From there they would go out to serenade the girls they liked. I could hear them the minute they started setting up the marimba in the street. When the musicians began to play, my father would make grumbling noises. The next day he would tease me into telling him who my suitor had been. We never went outside when they were playing, like the movies always show. No. I would know who the boy was by the songs he played. At the dances we went to, each boy sang certain melodies, and I knew how to identify each suitor by his songs. A day or two after the serenade, I would see the boy and thank him, saying that he shouldn't have bothered. There were many nights that I would go to bed listening for the sound of the marimba outside my window.

I had several suitors in my youth, but there was a very special one who became a lawyer and moved to Mexico City where he entered the Supreme Court. He died from an appendix operation when he was still young.

Not too long ago I thought, "When I die, everyone's going to find out all my secrets!" I had a big stack of love letters! Finally I decided to put them in a container and set fire to them. But first I read them one last time and relived many moments. Some were beautiful, and others I thought, "Oh, how ridiculous!" But it was very exciting. After reading them all, I burned them, then collected the ashes and put them in a plastic bag. I told my sister Flor that on the day of my funeral she should put the ashes from the love letters in the box with my own ashes. That way I would always be back in my youth.

When I was twenty-eight years old I married a German man, Udo Nickel, who was a nationalized American. When he had problems in Germany after the Second World War, he went to Argentina and from there to the United States. He had studied to be an airline pilot. I met Udo in Mexico City through a friend who had married an American. Udo and I liked each other from the very start. We were engaged for a year, and when we married, I went to live with him in Houston. Udo was a very good person and introduced me to many friends. He offered me the opportunity to see much of the United States. After living in Houston for three years, Udo and I came to live in Tuxtla Gutiérrez, where my husband started a mechanic's shop. We had no children. We wanted them, but we couldn't conceive, even though we went to different doctors for help. Then, after four and a half years together, suddenly the marriage ended and Udo returned to the United States. He was a diabetic who didn't take care of himself, and he died about fourteen years after our separation.

After the divorce I returned home, and I'm still here today. I didn't lack for marriage offers. I would admire certain men and they would visit and send flowers. But I never came to feel that ardor that one should feel when thinking about marrying. I had not felt it even with the suitors who had written the love letters that I burned not long ago. But with Udo, yes, I had felt that intensity, that desire. I felt a great love for Udo.

I never married again. "Better alone than in bad company," I said to myself. My life would have been different if I had remarried, but I was left with a certain fear. I didn't want another deception. No. A deception like that can be painful.

I dedicated myself to caring for my parents. My father finally sold the ranch, which, in its day, was one of the best ranches in the whole state. Thank God that with my inheritance I've never had to worry about money. I've never needed a man to support me.

When my father passed away, he died in my arms. I was raising him up to give him his medicine. I put my arm under his head and he simply died in that instant. It was difficult but also beautiful. My mother died about ten years later. Her death was even harder for me because I was left like I am now, alone.

Now I live quietly. I've known how to fill my life with travel and my group of friends. I'm fortunate that my sister Flor lives across the street and we see each other two or three times a day. And I have a good vice: I love to read. One learns a lot from reading, and it keeps the mind occupied. I also like to sew. I make whatever my nieces want. I even change the style of my clothes. I also enjoy cooking for people, usually family. I tell them, "Come to eat a new dish that I learned to prepare from the TV." I enjoy that.

Of course, the changes we've seen in San Cristóbal make me sad. In spite of the fact that we have many things that we didn't used to have, with the little we had back then, we lived intensely and, most of all, wholesomely. The drugs and the drunkenness we have today didn't exist. The worst pranks we used to play as children were ringing doorbells and then running away. But now the diversions are not so wholesome. Now at eight o'clock at night I'm afraid to take a taxi alone. What if they kidnap me? I don't feel the liberty I once had. I realize the drugs are worldwide, but I think the contraband won't end until drugs are legalized.

I try to be an understanding woman with everyone. I've learned from life that you must respect each person. I get along with people of all ages. It gives me great satisfaction to have love in my heart. If it's in my power to help some-one, I will do it with pleasure. Sometimes, to help is to listen, to give advice, or, if the person feels down, to say to them, "Come, let's take a walk or let's see what we can do!" With that, the person often feels better. I have many friends who seek me out. I've never felt lonely, never. Until now, I've never felt de-pressed or sad. I think that has kept me healthy. I thank God every day that I wake up in good spirits and without pain.

It's not that I feel death near, but, yes, I think about it. I'm in good health, but I know that is no guarantee. If God put me here, at any moment he can come for me. Of death itself, I'm not afraid. I'm at peace. I've had a good life and I'm satisfied.

What I still want to do is to travel. Luckily, I've been to Europe and the United States. Now I would like to travel with my sister to Chile, Machu Pic-chu, Brazil, Argentina, and Uruguay. We travel well together. I hope we'll be able to go somewhere soon.

Francisca Gómez López

Francisca Gómez López

My parents came to San Cristóbal to find work, and that's how I came to be born here, sixty-three years ago. After my little brother died, I was the youngest in the family. I grew up with my parents and my two sisters.

I have good memories of my father. I remember that he hugged me and held me and brought me gifts of fruit. Sometimes he gave us money. When he had none, he gave us nothing. I don't remember that he ever hit us.

The one who suffered was my mother. It was the same story as always with men—alcohol. I remember that my father would come home drunk and would throw my mother out of the house. He'd throw us children out too, and we would all have to sleep outside.

When I was seven years old, my father died from drinking too much. With three daughters to take care of, my mother had to work hard to get ahead. All four of us had to work, sweeping, mopping, cleaning houses, in order to survive. My mother never remarried. She had learned her lesson. I lived with my mother for many years and have many beautiful memories of her.

San Cristóbal was very pretty back then, surrounded by beautiful green fields. Now it's just too big. Streets and streets of cement houses that all look alike. There are no more fields, no more trees.

When I was about eight or ten years old, my sister and I would go to the market at two o'clock in the morning, just two little girls all alone. There weren't any rapists, no marijuana, nothing like that. Nowadays I'm terrified to go out in the streets at ten o'clock at night.

There used to be a mill on Veinteocho de Agosto Street. My sister and I would go there early in the morning to grind our corn. The mill opened at four o'clock in the morning, but we would arrive an hour early. We would sit there, waiting to grind our corn, and no one ever bothered us. Men would pass by and say, "Good morning." That's all. We were always shown respect. That doesn't happen anymore. The problem is that people now have too many children.

In my time, we didn't have birth control pills. I used to drink lemon juice so that I wouldn't get pregnant. I just took my juice for eight days after the last day of my period, depending on my body temperature. That's what I did for many years.

My mother helped me and both of my sisters when we had our children out of wedlock. I got pregnant by a man who was employed in the same house where I worked. Once I became pregnant I didn't want to keep working there. I was sixteen years old. I didn't marry the man, but I did live with him for three years and we had one son. The relationship with the father of my son ended because of the same old story. He drank. And when he drank he became violent.

So I went to Mexico City with the new family I started working for. My mother didn't want me to take my son away, so he stayed with her in San Cristóbal. I came to visit them once a year.

Living in Mexico City was a big change for me, in some ways sad and in other ways happy. The sad part was that I missed my son and my mother. In the city there was no one but strangers. On the other hand, it made me happy that I had my paycheck. Each month I sent a little money to my mother. I stayed in Mexico City for five years. But I hardly saw anything of the city because I was stuck inside the house working all the time. Every once in a while I would go out to visit the Church of Guadalupe. That was it. There were some men I was attracted to, but I never had any intention of staying in the city, so I didn't get involved.

When I returned to San Cristóbal I met another man, but I didn't marry him either. We just lived together. We had a son and a daughter together. That man didn't drink, but he was very, very jealous. His jealousy was like a sickness. We were together for three years and then broke up. But he gave me a little allowance for the children until they turned eighteen.

Meanwhile, I worked cleaning houses and washing clothes. I lived with my children in one little room of my house and rented out the other rooms. I didn't mind living like that. Later, when my children grew up, I gave a room to each of them.

My first son lived with me until he was fifteen years old, and then I lost him. He simply walked out of the house one day. The first year I received news about him and knew that he was living in Mexico City with his father's family. Then he returned to San Cristóbal for a short while but soon left again. He sent me a postcard from Oaxaca and one from Puebla, and then he disappeared completely. I felt absolutely terrible for many, many years and thought about him all the time. But he just went away. His father tried to look for him, but no one could ever find him. Years ago I gave him up for dead.

I don't know if it's good or bad to believe in dreams. But seven years after my son disappeared, I dreamt that he entered the house and said hello to me.

"You haven't come for so long," I said.

"Yes, Mama. They didn't give me permission to come back home," he said.

"Why do you need permission to come home?" I asked him. "This is your house!"

And after I talked like crazy about so many things and asked him so many questions, he told me, "You want to know the truth? I'm dead."

"They killed you? Tell me, who killed you?" I asked. "Did they put you in jail?" He didn't answer me.

He came to me very calmly in that dream. He wasn't at all desperate. I talked to him some more and finally said, "So, if you're dead, then what do you want? Why did you come here?"

"I come to ask you to forgive me," he said.

So I told him, "The only one who can forgive you is God." Then I woke up.

That dream was very powerful. It was so real. And since then I've remained calm, as if he had really spoken to me. Those words, to me, were so important. "I come to ask you to forgive me." Yes, that dream was very powerful and very sad, but it was also like a miracle.

I believe that after a certain amount of time a dead person is given permission to settle something left undone during his life. They can't do it too quickly. In the dream my son said, "I wanted to come home, but they wouldn't let me." What did that mean? I don't know. Where did those words come from? "I come to ask you to forgive me." Who sent him? I believe that God is the one who sent him. Ever since I had that dream, when someone asks me about my son, I tell them, "My son is dead."

Later his father told me that our son was obsessed with robbing a bank. He had even asked his father a lot of questions about it. So I'm thinking that maybe he tried to rob a bank and was killed during the attempt. And since he wasn't carrying any identification, they just buried him somewhere.

I have nothing left of him. Why did he come to me in the dream to ask forgiveness? Bless the Lord! "Don't ask forgiveness from me," I told him. "Ask for forgiveness from those who can forgive you." Son, I hope that you're at peace now.

Then there's my other son. He always ran around with a bunch of tramps. First he got married and had a daughter. But then he divorced his wife. After that marriage ended, he had one girlfriend knocking on the door and another one in his room. He had a kind of desperate obsession that wouldn't let him leave women alone. And they all wanted him too. Since he was about to get his divorce, one of the women began to pressure him. She wanted him to marry her no matter what. But he had fallen in love with yet another woman. This one worked in his office. The first woman found out and told him, "If you marry somebody else, I'll kill myself!"

After she said that, something horrible happened. My son tried to commit suicide. One afternoon he drank a small bottle of rat poison. Then he called to me, got down from the bed, and kneeled in front of me. He said good-bye to me and cried. And asked for my forgiveness.

"Why are you doing this? Let's call the doctor!" I screamed.

"I don't know why I did it," he said. "But I took the poison and now I'm going to die!"

"Where is your social security card?" I asked. I took him to the hospital where they pumped out his stomach. He stayed in the hospital all that night. The next day he left and went to work as if nothing had happened. Later he told me, "I'm going to throw away the poison."

I talked to him and said, "Look, José Luis, why don't you leave those women alone? Go away to Tuxtla to live, far away from those tramps. I think that's the solution. Otherwise they're never going to leave you in peace. Quit your job and hide out here at home."

"You're right," he said. "I don't want to see those women anymore."

But they were always around. He'd go looking for them. And the women were fascinated with him. I said to myself, "Dear Lord, how am I going to take care of this boy?" It's impossible to keep an eye on a son like that.

So, a week later he did it again! A woman who worked at the checkout counter in the drugstore came by to tell me that he had bought rat poison that morning. "José Luis is carrying around a bag of poison," she said. "Be careful!"

When I got home around six o'clock that evening, he was in his room. I had left his food on the stove, and it was still there. He had the television on at full volume. At eleven o'clock it was still on. I was wondering if I should go to see about him, but then I thought that maybe he was in there with a woman. I yelled through his door, "Turn down the TV!"

That whole night I couldn't sleep well. I kept wondering if I should go to see about him. But, honestly, I didn't want to go yet. I wanted to sleep a little while longer. Around seven o'clock in the morning the television was still turned on loud. That's when I woke up and knew that something was really wrong. I said to myself, "Oh! If I open that door and find him dead ... no, no, no ... better that he just stays there!"

After a while I got up and knocked two or three times on his door but heard nothing. I made him some oatmeal and then knocked again three or four times. Then I opened the door, and because it was a thin door, it opened easily. When I saw him lying there, I shook him and screamed, "What happened? What happened? What's wrong with you? Wake up! Oh! You're gone, you're gone! I don't want to see such a horrible thing! You've killed yourself! You've killed yourself! You took your own life!" I just didn't understand why he did it.

I felt such a tremendous anger that when the doctor came, I told him, "See if you can find a hole somewhere to put him in!" I was furious. When I went into his room later I saw the bottle of poison on his table. The doctor said that he had been dead for hours. He was already cold. Cold.

For a long time after my son was gone, I felt so much anger. Now it's not so strong. It's been five years since he died, and it has been a very hard time for me. I've dreamt that he's here at home. But I haven't had a dream like the one I had about my other son. I've finally forgiven him. But I blame that tramp who threatened to kill herself over him. She really didn't care about my son.

My son's daughter, my granddaughter, lives with her mother. The woman has another husband now, and they never bring the girl to see me. And I'm certainly not going to walk into their house to look for her.

My daughter and her two sons live with me now. Her husband travels around a lot. What do I know! That's not any concern of mine. That's her life. The only things that keep me going are my two grandsons. One is eight, and the other is fourteen years old. They are what I most enjoy in life.

You see, my mother died five months ago. She was ninety-something years old. She lived alone, but my sister and her three daughters lived next door. For a long time she wasn't able to eat well. Everything upset her stomach. Many days I would take her something to eat in the afternoon. It was important to me that she never lacked for food. She didn't take medicine because she didn't like it. When she first got sick, I was having chest pains and couldn't go out to see her. It hurt me to see her so sick. But, thank God, the day she died I went to see her at six o'clock in the morning. It was a Monday. When I first saw her, it seemed that she was unconscious, but I held her in my arms. I was with her when she died early that day. I held her and sang to her. She moved her lips along with me. She died singing! That's one thing that fills me with joy. I sang to her, caressed her face, and thought, "Let her sing! Let her sing!"

There are people who suffer a lot in this life. I see them and listen to what they have to say. And I think, "What do I have to complain about?" I haven't lost my strength or my capacity to make life pleasant. God is here with me, so I'm not alone. When I can, I like to go to the old folks' home and spend time with the sick. I spend a few minutes with each one. I listen to them talk about their lives. When they have something wrong with their stomachs, I tell them, "Take this herb." I would like to do more, give even more time and energy to the old people, but that's all I can do. I really like to be with them. I like to groom them and clean up after them. It doesn't disgust me. The other day a woman dirtied the hallway and I cleaned up the floor after her. The nurse said to me, "Why are you doing that when it's my job?" I told her that I like to look after them. The Lord tells me that I should do it. And I have the capacity to do it. I feel calm when I'm in the old folks' home. It gives me peace to do good deeds.

It's important not to keep that hate and that bitterness inside. That's all over now. If I had wallowed in self-pity after all that I've lived through, I would be dead. I made the decision that even with all this pain I don't want to be bitter. If I let myself get down, I won't be able to make it. It's hard, very hard, but I can get through it. I lost my sons and now my mother is gone. The thing that hurts most is my son's suicide. That pain will never go away. But I'm at peace because I know it wasn't my fault.

So that's the story of my life. Now I'm left with my grandsons, my daughter, and God. I have a good job as a cook in a nice restaurant here in town. There's nothing else to do but work.

Life has taught me that we just have to live it. We have to live it to the fullest. I'm here for a reason. I have thought about my own death, and I've told the Lord that I don't want to live as long as my mother did. My daughter works, and I don't want to be left at home alone.

I've learned many things in life, many little secrets. One thing I know is that it's bad to have mirrors in your bedroom. It's not common knowledge, but it's bad for your life in every respect. Mirrors in the bedroom rob people of their energy. And in front of the bed—even worse! When someone's going through hard times and complains to me, I tell them, "Take down those mirrors!"

I have a little mirror in my bedroom and every night I tell my grandson, who sleeps with me, "Take the mirror and put it face down." That's his routine each night before going to bed. If it's really true about the mirrors, then you've got to do it! I don't say that it's for sure, but those who know say so. I always listen to the psychologists on the TV and on the radio. Then I say to myself, "I'm going to do what they say!"

For me, that thing about the mirrors is absolutely true.

Manuela Ramírez Gómez

Manuela Ramírez Gómez

I think I'm at least seventy years old. I was born in Venustiana Carranza after the Mexican Revolution.

My mother was a good woman, and we got along well. She was a weaver, and I learned everything from her.

About my father—who knows! Yes, I knew my father, but I don't remember anything about him. I don't even remember how my parents got along, but they always stayed together.

I got married when I was thirteen years old. It used to be different, not like now. These days, youngsters fall in love and are always kissing. Back then, there was none of that falling in love and kissing stuff. Even though I wasn't in love when I married, I lived with my husband for forty years. He died sixteen years ago. That was fine with me.

I never thought about looking for another man. Heaven forbid! If you go off with another one who has a lot of money, you think that maybe he'll be better. You think, "This is the one! I'll go with this one. He's better!" But forget better. He'll be bad too, and then you'll end up with nothing at all. No, I never wanted another man and still don't. I put up with my husband for a long time, and since he's been gone, my life has been much, much happier. But when my husband died, I was left with five children, four girls and one boy. I called to God and asked him, "How am I going to live now?" Somehow I did it. What did I need a man for? Heaven forbid!

I'm always doing my weaving, doing my work. I still make my own thread. People don't know how to make and treat thread like I do. They just buy thread already made by a machine. But you can tell the difference. The thread that's made by hand is much finer. Yes, my thread is much better. It's very, very thin. See, here's the cotton, and this is the thread I made from it. It takes many days for me to spin enough thread for just one blouse. Then I have to boil the thread in corn *atole* to make it strong, so that it doesn't break. Then I dry it and separate each thread from the others. Next, I put together my loom and begin to weave my cloth. It's all so much work.

My blouses are very fine, like gauze. I also make the thick white men's pants that are typical of my town, the ones that have the brocaded designs in the form of a figure eight. First I weave the cotton cloth and then I sew the pants.

I weave, wash my clothes, cook my food, and go shopping for what I need. That's what I do every day. What else am I going to do but work? From the money I earn, I buy my coffee. With my work I can buy my corn and beans and my soft drinks. But it's a lot of work just to get paid.

When I was young, everyone dressed in traditional clothes. Nowadays they don't wear their traditional dress very often, and there's not much work. Even though people sometimes come down from San Cristóbal to buy, I'm always looking for new places to sell my things. When I'm working and selling well, my heart is happy.

My eyesight is still very good. But I have good days and bad days. I have diabetes, just like my daughter. I take medicine for it. Sometimes I'm well, and sometimes I'm not. Sometimes I eat, and other times I don't. On good days I feel like making thread and weaving. On bad days I don't feel like working or even living.

Only our Lord knows when we'll go. But I don't want to die yet. When I can make my thread and weave and sell my things I'm happy. And I still have much more work to do. My weaving is all that I have. My work saves me.

Natividad Elvira Pineda Gómez

Natividad Elvira Pineda Gómez

My father was a cattleman, just like all the men who had land back then. But when Venustiano Carranza came to Chiapas, he did away with the rich landowners. I was born on Guadalupe, my father's ranch near Ocosingo, on September 5, 1905. I lived through every bit of the Mexican Revolution.

Even before that, I saw the punishment handed down by Don Porfirio Díaz when he was still in power. Someone had put my father's mule into a corral full of cattle, but, of course, the two animals don't get along. Mule hide is tender and cattle horns are very sharp. The cattle gutted the poor mule and left him for dead. But who put the mule in the corral? The cattlemen from a neighboring ranch put him there. Why had they killed my father's mule? Who knows? But, of course, my father wanted the men arrested.

In those days they didn't put offenders in jail. If they were too old to fight, yes, they went to jail. But if they were young, then off to battle they would go. If they were criminals, well, with better reason. During the war, they would put criminals on the front lines where they would be the first ones killed. That was the punishment Porfirio Díaz handed out. I don't know how old I was then, but I remember seeing the mule and the cattle, and that scene has stuck in my mind all these years. But all that happened before the Revolution.

Much later, my uncle fought against the government. My uncle, my father's older brother, was General Carlos Alberto Pineda Ogarrio. He was a revolutionary who fought against Venustiano Carranza.

Just imagine! First came the Revolution and then came a famine like you wouldn't believe. People were falling dead of hunger in the streets. Thieves even murdered families so they could steal the corn from their fields.

After that, when I was around thirteen years old, came the Spanish influenza epidemic. All the houses were closed up tight, and no one went outdoors. The cattle were stomping in their corrals because there was no one to let them out. The sheep were bawling, the pigs were squealing from hunger. I think that epidemic happened all over Mexico. It was just terrible!

As I said, three things happened, one right after the other—the war, the famine, and the influenza epidemic. Many, many people died.

We lived on our ranch until the end of the Revolution. When we had to leave Guadalupe, we moved to El Pedernal, the ranch that belonged to my grandfather. That's where I grew up and where I grew old. It wasn't until recently that I came to live in San Cristóbal.

All my life I've been a rancher, because I liked living on a farm. I had chickens, turkeys, sheep, and cows. I would go into the corral, milk the cows, and take the milk to the kitchen. Then I'd strain it and boil it for breakfast. I would leave the rest, separating the cream, so that by two o'clock in the afternoon I'd have rennet to make my cheese. Delicious!

I began to bake cakes and pastries when I was around sixteen years old. But I don't remember how old I was when I first scrambled eggs or cooked a pot of beans. I don't remember because I began to cook when I was very little. My mother put me in the kitchen, and I liked it. The truth is, I love to cook. All my life I've loved to be in the kitchen.

I never learned to read or write. I didn't want to go to school. Oh, I started to learn my letters, so I do know the alphabet. But when we began to add numbers—Heaven forbid! How was I ever going to learn that? I didn't like school at all. But everything that I wanted to learn I just had to see once and it stayed with me. I always remember what I need to do for each dish and how much of each ingredient I need to add. All of my recipes are in my head.

I can make so many delicious things. For example, here's a tasty chicken dish. First, fry a chicken until it's tender, then take the meat from the bone and cut it into pieces. When the pieces are golden brown, add onion, garlic, oregano, thyme, whole black pepper, raisins, olives, almonds, and a little vinegar and sugar. Once you've put in the vinegar, liquefy a few tomatoes and add them to the pan, along with two or three sliced zucchinis and some green beans. And then, about half an hour before it's done, add a big cup of brandy. Always make sure the pan is covered so that the wonderful smell doesn't evaporate. And make sure you stir it often. This makes a very delicious dinner.

Not too long ago someone wrote down everything and made a cookbook of my recipes. I don't remember the title of the book, but it has all my traditional dishes from Chiapas. My book was presented to the public just last year. They gave me a big party in the park in front of the municipal building and announced on the loudspeaker, "NOW THE COOKBOOK OF MISS NATIVIDAD PINEDA GÓMEZ WILL BE PRESENTED!" Musicians played the marimba. Then they set off all the fireworks they had on hand.

Soon I'll celebrate my one-hundredth birthday, but I keep doing the things I always did, like teaching. I will teach as long as God gives me life and I can go on. Just because I'm old, I won't forget what I have to do. I teach people to make cakes and pies, hams and all kinds of sausages. Well, to those who want to learn. The problem is that right now not too many people want to learn. And they can't afford to pay for the classes. Some people are interested. Others say, "Who cares?" We all don't have the same tastes, you know. Nowadays the youngsters are just too rebellious. They halfway make bread, and with that, they're satisfied. They don't want to excel in anything. They don't have any enthusiasm at all.

One day a lady asked me to give a class. "Okay, I'll go," I said. But from the beginning I didn't like the place because the kitchen was too small.

Then they told me, "Look, if you want to teach here, you have to come early to sweep the floor, clean the tabletop, and wash the pots and pans."

I listened to what they were saying. Then I said, "I don't work like that. Wherever I teach, I want to find the kitchen clean, swept, and the dishes already washed and ready to use."

When everything was ready for the class, I began to knead the dough. But the students were just sitting there, doing nothing. Well, I don't teach like that. The ones who are learning have to knead, beat, and stir. They learn by doing. If someone else does it for them, they'll never know how to do it right.

When recipes are written down in books, I feel like an idiot. I have to ask someone to read them to me. And when the recipe says, "One cup of flour, one cup of milk," well, what I want to know is, what size cup do I use? A quarter liter? A half liter? A liter? What cup are they talking about? There are big cups, tiny cups. So how am I supposed to know? They have to give me the exact measurements so I can make the dish correctly. I don't like to cook with recipes written down on paper.

Sometimes when I hear that they're giving cooking classes on television, I like to watch them. But normally I don't watch TV. When I hear the recipe just once I can remember it. With the grace of God, ever since I was little I've had a gift for cooking.

When we lived on the ranch, my grandmother made a vegetable wax that we used for making candles. She cut up a certain plant she found in the forest and then boiled it to make a wax that looked a little like cooking grease. She made candles with that wax. So I tried to make them too. But do you know how they came out? As if they had chickenpox! My poor candles always turned out ugly. I could never make them right. Never. But food, yes. I always made delicious food.

Another thing my grandmother made was chewing gum. She would cut the chicle tree, and the gum would come out in little grains that looked like coffee beans. After washing the grains, she would soak them in limewater— just like the limewater you soak the corn in when you make tortillas. She'd boil the grains until they got thick, then turn them out on the kitchen table and knead them until she had a ball of chewing gum.

I also learned to make black soap from ashes and lime. You take a gallon of beef or pork fat and mix it with ten measures of ash for one liter of lime. Then you mix it really, really well. First you have to add a little water so that it stays moist. Then you pour it into molds.

I learned to make sweet beer when I was young. No one makes it much anymore because it's a lot of work, even though it's pretty easy to do. If you add too much sugar, it will turn thick, like egg whites, and then it's ruined. Well, it's okay to drink it like that as long as you don't have diabetes. But it really shouldn't be thick. It should be as clear as water. And it has to be just right, not too sweet, not too bitter. You cork the bottle and tie it with a string. Then you let it sit in the sun for ten days. Sometimes when it's sitting in the sun it will ferment, and the cork will pop right off and go POC! Then all your beer will fly out!

I never got married. I fell in love a few times and considered it. But then I thought, many women end up hurt and all beaten up. Or their husbands leave them with a bunch of children, and they're left alone with the responsibility. The men don't care, and so they run off. I didn't want any part of that. So I kept thinking about it. Meanwhile, I was busy working on the ranch and the time kept passing. After a few years I thought, "What's the point?" First our parents order us around, and after them, God has the word. Many men are much too bossy. I know where I want to go, what time to go out, and what time to come back. No one tells me what to do. No one owns me.

Life is much easier like this. I go wherever I would like to pass the time. If I want to go to work, I just tell my little sister, Refugio. I've lived with my sister all my life.

We moved to San Cristóbal long before the Zapatista Uprising started. Look, I just want to say something about that. First of all, those rebels made a lot of racket. But if you notice, it just stirred up a bunch of lies. The Zapatistas were completely against the government, and when they came into town they attacked the municipal building. That's where they went to cause problems. They didn't enter the houses. They didn't kill people in the streets. So why is everyone talking so much? People should tell the truth and not make such a big deal out of it.

Anyway, we came to San Cristóbal because of my rheumatism. Then a few years ago I broke my hip. I was on my way to six o'clock mass at the cathedral. I told my sister that I was going to take a taxi, but she said, "Don't waste your money. I'll walk with you to the church."

"But what if a car runs over us?" I asked her.

"I'll take care that nothing happens to you," she assured me.

But the first thing we did was stumble and fall just outside the church. To make matters worse, my sister fell on top of me. I fell right on my seat and immediately knew that I had broken my hip. Since then, I've been completely useless to anyone. It's hard for me to even take a step. My bones seem stuck, and I don't have strength in my legs. That fall ruined me.

Look, if death comes to me, it's God's will and I won't feel sad. When it comes, it will be the light that comes to all of us sooner or later. I used to be a little afraid, and I would say to myself, "I'm going to die, but I hope not for a long time." But now the light and the hour that I must go are coming near. Who gets to stay in this world? Nobody.

There's one important thing to remember. As long as we behave well and we're in God's grace, our soul will always be his. Now if we're really bad, then we'll go to hell. But God is our Lord. Every day I recite a prayer that they say will help me pass directly into heaven. I won't even have to pass through purgatory. The prayer goes like this:

> Oh, my great Jesus, creator of the human species,
> rest your eyes on us who kneel before your altars.
> We are yours and yours we want to be.
> We devote ourselves of our own free will
> to your most sacred heart.
> There are many who don't know you,
> and many who reject your commandments.
> Have pity on us, most venerable Jesus,
> draw us to your sacred heart.
> Rule like a king over the unfaithful.
> Reign over your prodigal sons who have abandoned you.
> Call them home to the house of their Father
> so that they will suffer no hunger or misery.
> Rule like a king over the misconduct and discord
> of those who have drifted away from you.
> Return them to the unity of faith,
> the safe harbor of truth,
> so that soon there will be one flock and one shepherd.
> Teach those who are still lost
> in the old superstitions of paganism.

Take them out of the darkness and guide them
to the light of the kingdom of God.
Give to your church, O Lord,
everlasting freedom and happiness.
Grant peace and union to all people.
Glory to the divine heart in which all is well.
He is alone in glory and honor.
World without end, forever and ever. Amen.

The Bible says that he who recites this prayer with devotion during his entire life will neither touch the flames nor feel the heat of purgatory. That's why I believe I will go directly to heaven. I have God in my heart, and that is what will save me.

One day I was out giving my classes. It was late, and I was ready to go home. A man drove up in his car and offered me a ride. On the way home he asked me, "And what religion are you?"

"Catholic," I told him. "My parents, grandparents, and great-grandparents have always been Catholic. Why should I go astray? I believe what my family has always believed."

"Oh, no!" he said. "You're really lost, lady."

"And why is that?" I asked.

"Remember back when people weren't educated and there was just one lawyer in town and everybody went to that lawyer? Or just one doctor in town and everyone went to that doctor? Now there are lots of doctors and lawyers. You go to the one you like the best. That's the way it works with our belief in God. There are many religions. We don't believe in what others tell us to believe but in what our heart tells us."

"Look," I said, "I believe in the Lord and nobody's going to change that."

Well, the man got so mad that he made me get out of his car and left me standing on the street corner. He didn't even take me home!

My family has always been Catholic. No one is going to make me lose my way. I am what I am. End of story.

Sebastiana Pérez Espinoza

Sebastiana Pérez Espinoza

The first time I remember being happy was when I was around three years old and my mother and father said, "This girl is going to be named Sebastiana, after her grandmother." My grandmother was a wonderful person. We all adored her, and so I was delighted to be named after her. From then on, my parents wouldn't let anyone hit me. How would anyone dare to hit the beloved Sebastiana! They said, "With this name, no one will ever bother you." I felt that my grandmother's name protected me.

When I was growing up, my parents would say, "If Sebastiana misbehaves, we'll have to pull her ears." But I was always good and worked hard, so they never had to punish me.

I was born in 1941 in the municipality of Chilón, one of fifteen children. My father worked on a coffee plantation. He drank a lot, and when he got drunk he hit us. We used to tremble with fear when he was around. But when my father was sober, he and my mother were very close and the whole family was happy. My parents made us laugh and loved us very much.

I used to have to carry around my baby brothers even when I was very young. The baby was heavy and sometimes I fell down, baby and all. My mother would get mad at me then. But she was a good mother and fed us and gave us everything she could. She gave us all her heart. She taught us how to do the chores, how to wash clothes, make tortillas, and grind corn on the metate.

But she didn't know how to do *luch*, the cross-stitch embroidery that is typical of this area. Since I wanted to learn, I studied the embroidery work of other women to see how they made the stitches. And eventually I learned to embroider by myself.

The best days of my childhood were when the family was all together and we had more food than usual. When we ate well, life was happy and we had good times. Sometimes my father would take us to Chilón to eat meat. First my parents would feed me and my brothers and sisters, then my father would eat, and finally my mother.

When I was twelve or thirteen years old, they put me to work. The whole family worked in the fields, sowing and harvesting beans and corn, carrying rocks, and burning lime. I was a good worker and liked doing physical labor.

I knew from the example of my parents that when a woman gets married she will have to work very hard. I also knew that soon after men marry they begin to drink. I felt in my heart that men were not the only ones who were given hands with which to work. I knew how to do things. I could work too! I knew that I was able to get what I needed all by myself. I didn't need a man to take care of me. I didn't want to have my mother's life, so I never fell in love and never got married.

Ever since I was very young, I've dreamed about the Lord. In one dream I saw rocks in a river, and under one of them I found a bright, shining coin. I interpreted this as a sign from God to join him.

Another night I dreamt that the Virgin Mary was standing in the middle of the road. She said to me, "Where are you going?"

"I'm going home to see my mother," I answered.

"Here I am. I'm waiting for you," she told me.

"I want to go with you. Take me," I begged.

But she said, "You can't go right now. You still have a great deal of work to do."

"I can't do more than I'm already doing, dear Mother," I cried.

"Yes, you can do it. You can!" she insisted. "I have so much work, and I need you to help me. I will hand the women over to you. There are so many women who are suffering. You, Sebastiana, are going to care for them."

"But I want to go right now," I told her.

"Wait a little while," she said. "I will come to get you later. First do your work. I hand the women over to you."

I began to cry, and the Virgin said, "Go home now to see your mother."

So I went, and the Virgin followed me. We walked together until I saw my sister walking below. Suddenly a huge rock fell on top of her and crushed her. I screamed, "Look, dear Mother! My sister!"

"Oh well," said the Virgin. "We must all go sometime. We all must die."

That's when I woke up from my dream. I got up quickly to say my prayers. That dream showed me the way to deliver my heart.

One day the Sisters of the Divine Shepherd came to our community to speak, and they really impressed me. Later, in 1973, the Sisters invited me to a conference in San Cristóbal, and I went to hear what they had to say. They talked to us about religion and about women's lives. After hearing them speak, I kept going back to look for the Sisters. My parents gave me permission to go to other conferences and other meetings, and that's how I came to join the Sisters of the Divine Shepherd here in Chilón. By then my father had stopped drinking, and life at home was much calmer. When I decided not to get married and to live with the Sisters, my mother and father approved. They told me, "It's wonderful that you're going to join the Sisters. You'll learn so much. They'll teach you things that we don't know and then you can come to teach us!"

I traveled to Mexico City and to Guatemala to meet the Sisters there. I saw how they lived and how they managed their lives. Some women can live the religious life and others can't. Each person has her own feelings and her own way of thinking. For some, this path is too hard, and so they're not forced to join. As for me, I learned how to give my heart to service in the communities.

In 1976 I formed my own congregation, the Younger Sisters of the Divine Shepherd. No one had ever formed a group of Tzeltal Indian nuns. I did it because I was looking for a way of helping the women who suffer, a way of saving them. In some families, parents and children live in harmony and lack for nothing. But other women are burdened with problems. This has always been the most important part of our work. We try to help married women who have husbands who drink and children who live in pain. There are many Tzeltal women who are single, who have left their husbands and children because of problems with alcohol. We talk to the women about how they can recover their lives, how each one can be happier in their homes, how they can find a way to live with less suffering.

In the past, indigenous women were afraid to leave their communities. Their husbands told them they didn't have the right to leave. But since the Zapatista Movement began in 1994, the lives of some women have changed a little. They are learning that they do have rights. And if they want, they can do things differently. But not all the men allow their wives to go out and do things on their own.

We inform the women about many subjects. Some of us go to the communities to promote health. We pick medicinal plants in the wild and then prepare them for our patients in the villages. I learned to cure with herbs from my father, who was a healer. We also show the women how to grow vegetables and medicinal herbs, and we buy chickens so that women can start their own chicken farms. There's always a lot of work to do.

I used to walk to the communities, but now I work at the cooperative here in Chilón where we make embroidered blouses, bags, backpacks, and rugs. In the co-op we are making a little money. People who are familiar with our work sometimes give us a donation, which is a great help. We have our house and a new kitchen. God helped us with all this, but we still need many things. All in all, we're doing well.

Ever since I joined the congregation I've been very happy. There are twelve of us now, of all ages, in the Younger Sisters of the Divine Shepherd. But there are some companions who don't like this life because they don't earn much money. Sometimes we don't have enough to eat, and they find the life with us too hard. Some have left the congregation and gone back to their homes. But I've withstood all the difficulties of the religious life.

What worries me most is that I don't know how to read or write. We are invited to conferences in other states, but only two of us know how to speak Spanish. They're the only ones who can go. The rest of us can't communicate because we only speak Tzeltal. What we most need is to learn Spanish and to learn more about accounting. We want to study and learn more, but the majority of us didn't even finish grammar school.

If I had it all to do over, I would do everything just the same. What makes me happiest is the Lord, our only Father, who listens when we're in pain. It is he who makes me happy. All day and every day he is in my heart.

Dilery Penagos Gutiérrez

Dilery Penagos Gutiérrez

I was born on September 3, 1936, in San Cristóbal de las Casas, in my family's house on Real de Guadalupe Street. I spent my childhood on this block, which we have shared with our neighbors in such a special way that we all feel like family. We've seen some friends grow old and leave us, and we've come to know the new generations. We have experienced childhood, youth, married life, and old age together.

I'm the second child of four siblings from a good family. We were all very close. Our way of looking at life—the rules, customs, and education that our parents gave us—has been our foundation. I believe it's important to form a home with love and respect. In reality, life has its challenges. It has its beautiful parts and its hard times. But overall, with a base of love and respect, even when you're confronted with especially difficult situations, you're able to get through them.

When I was little, my parents gave me permission to go out in the afternoons and have fun with the neighborhood children. We jumped rope and played with our dolls. On Sundays the family would go to Peje de Oro for a picnic in the country. It was a beautiful walk, and the river there was crystal clear. The trip back from our outing was wonderful too. Passing through Cuxtitali, we would always stop to buy pork rinds, because my father loved them.

There were fiestas in all the barrios—La Merced, Guadalupe, Cuxtitali, El Cerrillo, Mexicanos, and San Ramón. There were sweets and breads and balloons. Fireworks announced each fiesta. Every year, on the third of May, our family and friends would climb the hill to the Church of Santa Cruz to celebrate the Day of the Holy Cross.

When the weather was cold, we would have *lunadas* in the street at night. Families would build a bonfire and sing, drink fruit punch, and cook meats on the grill. It's a custom that has not been lost. But the town was much quieter then. People were already in their houses at seven o'clock, and by nine o'clock the streets were deserted.

There were very few cars in San Cristóbal, and at first they were a great novelty. Transportation had always been by horse. Real de Guadalupe Street was paved with beautiful stones. It was the custom in our neighborhood to sweep the stones each day. When the grass between them grew too high, we would cut it back so that the stones were always clean.

Several years ago, when the street was being repaired, the workmen ripped up the pavement. I was happy to see that the original stone was still under the cement. I took some of those stones and put them around my red bougainvillea. They're in my garden now as a reminder of that beautiful part of my childhood.

San Cristóbal has changed because of the population that has moved in from nearby towns and from other parts of Mexico. With this growth have come new customs. Even so, I think that we still preserve much of the traditional ways. San Cristóbal has its own special flavor. We still go to the outdoor market instead of the superstores. The beauty of shopping in the market is incomparable.

Over the years, foreigners have left a very special mark on our city. When we were children, it was so exciting to see Doña Gertrudis Blom pass by with her beautiful Afghan dogs. Trudi was an imposing character. You couldn't help but notice that she was someone special. She was outgoing and friendly and knew how to create a presence with her unique clothes and jewelry. She even dyed her hair different colors. Nowadays the young people dye their hair red, orange, or blue. But in those days, what a novelty it was to see Doña Trudi with her short hair dyed in tones of burgundy, red, blue, and pink. She was so beautiful.

Doña Trudi often came to our house to visit and to buy antiques from my mother. She and my mother had a wonderful friendship and shared the same ideas, interests, and tastes. My mother loved to talk with her because Trudi was an encyclopedia of knowledge. Her husband, Frans, who was always so quiet, probably knew more about the Maya culture and the Lacandons. But after his death Trudi took his place. She had a great capacity for learning.

I met my husband, who was originally from Jiquipilas, here in San Cristóbal. We had five children, two sons and three daughters. When our children were still babies, my husband went back to school to obtain a degree in law—quite an achievement. Later I had the opportunity to start my own arts and crafts business, which I've had now for thirty-six years.

My five children have been a very important part of my life. My husband and I have enjoyed watching them grow up and marry. Now we are beginning a new stage of our lives, alone for a while until the house fills with grandchildren. I would like to continue working as long as I have health, strength, and the disposition. It's something that, instead of complaining about, I really enjoy. Work keeps you in shape and gives you the possibility of doing the things that you want to do.

My mother was an outgoing and interesting person who had a positive way of looking at life. Many people remember her because of the gift she had with people. She was one of the greatest treasures that could have been given to me. And so her death was impossible for me to accept. She had cancer and fought valiantly against it. It was difficult for me to see my mother, who had such high spirits, such joy and dynamism, go downhill. After many treatments of all kinds in Mexico City, there was nothing else that could be done for her but to bring her back to San Cristóbal. Here is where she wanted to die. But in 1980, the year she passed away, a tremendous hurricane had destroyed the highways. She wasn't allowed on an airplane because of the seriousness of her condition. So we had to bring her in an ambulance over those horrible roads. When we got as far as La Ventosa, in Oaxaca, her condition worsened. The trip was agonizing, but we talked to her calmly, saying, "We're almost there, just a little farther and we'll be home."

My father's death was also difficult, but at least my mother was still with us then. Her presence was a salve that helped ease the pain. But when she passed, it was very hard on us. To this day, her death has been one of the toughest things I've had to endure.

I'm not really afraid of anything, because that's the way I am. I was more fearful when I was younger, but not anymore. Even during the Zapatista

Uprising in 1994, I felt no fear. Since we didn't know what was happening, I felt curiosity more than anything else. It was even entertaining. When the Zapatistas took over the municipal building, my children and I went downtown to see Sub-Commander Marcos and all of his men, who appeared to be totally exhausted. Thinking back, it's hard to believe that all of that really happened. But I was never afraid.

Maybe I fear death. At my age a health problem like high blood pressure may upset me sometimes and make me fearful. But it's just another experience in life. I ask God to give me the peace that I may need to understand that death is a step I'll have to take sooner or later. There should be no reason for me to be afraid to confront my end. Maybe it's something like giving birth; others tell you about it, but until you experience it yourself, you'll never understand how it really is. The important thing is to have complete confidence in God, to leave our lives in his hands. Death is a normal part of life. All of us will go there eventually.

I have lived during a significant era of humanity. When man landed on the moon, we were on that adventure with them. It seemed unreal! How could it be? A man on the moon! The fall of the Berlin Wall really impressed me and filled me with joy. And all the marvelous advances in science and communications— television, satellites, computers, laser operations, space travel. They were things that we saw in science fiction movies and now they're a reality. There were many tragic events but many more that have made our lives richer.

We are beautified by all of the people around us. Even the Zapatista Uprising has left us with important messages. Maybe the time is right to compensate for some things that perhaps were not correct. During the time that Don Samuel Ruiz was bishop, there were many changes here. I was eighteen years old when he first came to San Cristóbal. We Coletos had been brought up in a traditional ideology, and Don Samuel changed that a little. Those traditional ideas weren't all bad. It seems that we just had different points of view. If it had not been for him, we would still be following a way of life that wasn't always proper. We will have to analyze it, don't you think? I'm not going to deny that I've lived in a time when the treatment of Indians has not been the most just. But in my family's case, and particularly in my case, our father taught us to respect the Indians. They were our clients. Each of us had our own place.

Today San Cristóbal is much more open than it was in my youth. The townspeople used to be more select and close-minded. Little by little, things have changed. Our church has the capacity to communicate. But in the past, no one even spoke to the Protestants. Now the mentality has changed for the better, we hope.

We are living at a very special moment. When the first Protestant pastors came here, San Cristóbal was 90 percent Catholic. Now we are only 60 or 70 percent Catholics. San Cristóbal has been barraged by many new sects and religions.

My principles, my religious formation, make me grateful to God for every day of life, for everything that I have. They say that life is a cornfield through which everyone must pass. You just have to enter and go through it, but you'll never be able to repeat the passage. You have one chance, that's all. It's up to you to choose what you want. Perhaps you don't always make the best choice, but it's your decision. That is what fills life with many wonderful memories.

When people ask me if I ever thought of leaving San Cristóbal, I say, perhaps, yes, I could have. But why? I've been so happy here.

Micaela Díaz Díaz

Micaela Díaz Díaz

I really don't know how old I am. I was born in a little Tzotzil hamlet about a half hour from San Andrés Larrainzar. I hardly remember my parents at all because my mother died when I was six years old. There were seven children in our family, and after my parents died, my oldest sister raised us. She taught me everything I know about life, but she's been gone now for many years. Just me and one of my sisters are left.

My oldest sister taught me to weave the *huipiles* that San Andrés women wear every day. She taught me how to treat and clean the wool, how to spin and embroider with it. When I was a little girl, we still dressed in *huipiles* made of wool. That's all changed. Our *huipiles* are now made of pure cotton.

Besides weaving our clothes, we worked in the fields. We grew our corn, beans, and vegetables. We had chickens, and we also took care of our sheep. Growing up, we had enough food, enough of everything. My sister took good care of us, and our lives weren't so bad.

There was no school nearby, so I never learned to read or write. But I did learn to weave very well. We lived far away from everything and hardly ever saw anyone but family. It was something special to go to the market on Sundays. We bought what we needed and talked to the people. We also enjoyed going to the fiestas in town.

I married when I was around sixteen years old. I was really in love, but I'm embarrassed to tell you what it was I liked about my husband. I never had children, and that's why he looked for another woman. My husband said to me, "You know what? You can't give me children, so I'm going to look for someone who can." So I told him, "Well, go look for her, then."

And that's just what happened. But I didn't want him to go, so we had horrible fights. He hit me again and again because I didn't want him to leave me. And now when I remember those fights, it breaks my heart and I start to cry.

My husband did find another wife and went to live with her. But he didn't have any children with her either. She already had a son with another husband. But not long after they were married, her first husband became very skinny and died. My husband came to see me and I told him, "You see, that woman is a man killer!" But he went back to her anyway.

He lived with that woman for six years, and each year he got thinner and thinner—skinny as a bone. And then he died in that woman's house. He deserved to die like that for going off with that evil woman!

She killed three husbands like that. She was one of those women who looks for a man, then kills him. Then looks for another man and kills him too. There were several men in our community who died just like that.

There were other men who wanted to get together with me, but I didn't want another husband. Sometimes men hit women. Sometimes they hit too much. And that's the truth. Without a husband, there's no one to hit or yell at you. So I never looked for another man. But I've never lived alone. There's always been family with me.

I've worked for twenty-eight years at Sna Jolobil, the Indian textile cooperative. Sna Jolobil was the first indigenous store in San Cristóbal. It opened in 1976. Back then, only men worked there, and many weavings were stolen. Someone had even stolen a very special *huipil* from Chamula.

One day Pedro Meza, the organizer of the co-op, asked me to come to work in the store for just a month or two. So I came to San Cristóbal and rented a room. I became the chief of security in the store. I did a good job, and soon there weren't so many robberies. I also sold my weavings and began to make some money.

In 1977 Indians weren't supposed to walk in the streets of San Cristóbal at night. We didn't have permission to live in town. Even though I was one of the first Indians who worked and lived there, I never had any problems.

I liked living in San Cristóbal and working in the store all those years. Now many Indian women work in Sna Jolobil.

My weavings are in the book *Living Maya*. And there are many photos and postcards of me all over the world. Yes, I'm a little famous, and that's fine with me. I like being famous.

I just moved back to San Andrés not long ago. I was tired of working. My legs hurt from standing so much. So Pedro Meza had the idea of retiring me, and he gave me a pension. I think it was a good idea to leave my work.

Now I enjoy planting my cornfield and my vegetables. When I get tired I can rest. I don't think much about dying, and I'm not afraid of death. When I'm dead, I'm dead and will be gone forever. Such is life.

In the last few years there have been some changes in Indian women's lives. Now many women look for their own husbands. When I was young, it wasn't like that at all. Men used to ask the mother and father for their daughter. It didn't matter whether she wanted to marry the man or not. Now women go all by themselves to look for their man. I don't think that's the way it should be done. There are many young women who don't respect their in-laws and don't obey them. Later, when the marriage doesn't work out, the parents say, "You see, daughter, you didn't do it right." I like the old customs much better.

Maruca Navarro, viuda de Alfonso

You know that phrase, "To remember is to live"? Well, for me it is "To remember is to suffer again."

I was born into a very wealthy family in San Cristóbal. There were many families with money back then, but there were no banks. People used to bury their money under a rosewood tree or hide it in holes in the walls or inside their home altars. Once a woman I knew who was lying on her deathbed kept pointing again and again to her altar. Relatives handed her one saint after another, but, no, she just kept pointing to her altar because that was where she had hidden the family's money.

I was General Utrilla's granddaughter. He was very wealthy even before he became governor. My aunt Cande, the youngest daughter of my grandfather, owned the entire block across from the Church of Santo Domingo, where the Utrilla house is now.

My father was Dr. Navarro. He was born in Guadalajara and came to live in San Cristóbal just by chance. There was a very rich woman named Doña Graciana who lived here in town. She became sick with the gall bladder and needed an operation, but no one here knew how to perform it. With much care, they carried Doña Graciana to the train in Arriaga and from there to Mexico City. My father was working in the hospital where they operated on her. He didn't perform the operation himself, but he did attend to her. After she recovered, the lady was ready to come home, but the doctors wouldn't release her unless she had someone to look after her. She offered my father very good money to accompany her back to San Cristóbal. My father accepted and later became like a son to her.

Doña Graciana was a very good friend of my grandfather's and often went to visit him. My father met my mother there in my grandfather's house. My mother was very beautiful and my father very handsome. They got along extremely well. They had ten children. I was the ninth one, born in 1915.

My grandfather died when I was two years old, so I only have a vague memory of him. After his death the family declined economically and socially.

I grew up in the Utrilla house and studied at the Steinpres School. I loved to study. A Guatemalan artist came to teach us, and by the age of twelve, I was painting oils. I still have some of those paintings.

Life then was pure joy. The Los Arcos mill and the Peje de Oro mill belonged to my family. On the weekends we would go walking out there, because the area was so beautiful.

After grammar school I wanted to keep studying, and my father finally gave me permission to enter the Modelo School. That was also a wonderful time in my life until, just before the end of the school year, my family was terribly shaken by the death of my brother. It was a severe blow. He was killed at La Enseñanza School because of a girlfriend he had there. He was eighteen years old, handsome and full of life, and I loved him very much. My brother Rodolfo, who was a doctor, had to do the autopsy, and it affected him so much that he died a few years later of a heart attack.

After that tragedy my father didn't want us to go back to school. But later, when things calmed down, he changed his mind. When I finished high school I studied typing and shorthand. Because my father was not originally from San Cristóbal, he didn't have such radically conservative ideas about how women were meant to stay home and take care of the house. He had somewhat more liberal ideas about such things.

I married Jorge Alfonso Molinares, whom I had met in high school when I was around eighteen years old. I fell in love with him because of the way he treated me and the kind of person he was. I still have two photos of our wedding. We lived in San Cristóbal for five years, and all of my children were born here.

During the sixth year of our marriage, the government promoted my husband to a higher position in the tax department, and we moved to the state capital, Tuxtla Gutiérrez. But every Sunday we'd come to San Cristóbal on the bus to visit my mother and my sister Amada, who never married.

With a better salary, Jorge bought a nice new car. But he didn't like to drive on the highway, so for our first trip in the car, Jorge hired a driver. When we arrived in San Cristóbal, Jorge told the driver that he could go for a walk while we visited my mother, but instead the driver went to have a few drinks. Around five o'clock in the afternoon he arrived, and we got in the car to return to Tuxtla.

The car was full because my sister Delfia and my mother decided to come with us. On a sharp curve we went over the side of the mountain and rolled until a tree stopped our fall. My mother was thrown from the car and died of a heart attack. My husband, Jorge, hit his head on a rock and died of a brain hemorrhage. Delfia broke her ribs, my little Flor broke her nose, and Ceci tore her scalp. I was gravely hurt. My femur jammed into my pelvis and damaged my vertebrae. I also had contusions on my head.

Some kindhearted people took us all to the hospital in Tuxtla. I hovered between life and death. In one second my life had changed forever. I became so depressed that I never left the house. I was in mourning for three years, wearing a black shawl, as is the custom here. Yes, a black shawl in the awful heat of Tuxtla!

A neighbor used his influence to help me get a pension, even though the accident had occurred on a Sunday, not during work hours. Finally the office paid me a pension of one hundred and seventy pesos a month. One hundred and seventy pesos for a family of five! That was only enough to pay the rent. My children grew up with hunger and always went around badly dressed. I had to be mother, father, maid, and everything to them.

I also had fifteen thousand pesos coming to me from a life insurance policy. Jorge's friends offered to help me start a gift shop with the money, but I was so injured I could hardly move. A safe containing our documents was in the office where my husband worked, but I was in such bad shape I couldn't remember the combination. They had to drill into the safe from the back to take out the documents.

That insurance money saved my life. A dear friend of Jorge's invested it at a high interest rate, and for the next twenty-five years he sent me a check once a month. It was three hundred pesos, and what an enormous help that was!

One day I caught a bad cold and had to go to the doctor. He told me, "You don't have a cold. It's an allergy. And it's not going away until you come out of mourning, or, at the very least, stop wearing black. Put on a white blouse and a black skirt, if you want. But the way you are now, all in black, the sun can't shine on you. You must get out in the sun!" And for certain, when I took off my mourning clothes and put on a white blouse I began to get well.

Later a friend of my brother's told me there might be a job opening up in the government. "I don't know how to do anything," I reminded him. But then I remembered the shorthand I had learned at school. "Good," he said. "Tomorrow I'll send you a machine." It was around the twentieth of August and the job started on the first of September. My fingers were clumsy, but I practiced day and night.

How I suffered those first days at work! I had never been in an office in my life. No one wanted to teach me or to help me with anything. And there was a good reason for that. If all the workers in the office had shared that job, they would have all gotten raises. But I was given the job instead, so everybody was mad at me. Every night I went home in tears and swore that I wouldn't return the next morning. But I had to return, out of necessity. I really needed that job, and I tried very hard to do my best. Eventually I earned merits for my work and was earning three hundred and twenty-five pesos a month. I ended up working there for ten years and put four thousand pesos in a savings account.

I never thought about remarrying. Yes, there were men who were interested in me, and they would come around to call. But I thought, "Why make my children suffer?" No, I never wanted to marry again.

My son Jorge deserves a lot of credit. Without a father or money or the ability to buy books, he would ride to school, hanging off the side of the bus. Later he left to study architecture in Mexico City. When it was time for my daughter Flor to choose her career, I asked, "What do you want to study, business or education?" Even though she didn't want to study teaching, she won gold medals three years in a row. My Flor is very intelligent! Alito studied accounting. When Ceci finished high school, she and I were alone in Tuxtla.

By then my children were living in Mexico City, and they sent for Ceci and me. Despite all the difficulties, I was finally happy in Tuxtla, and the change to Mexico City was very hard. But I started a new life there.

I lived in Mexico City for seventeen years. During that time, I went to Europe twice. On the first trip, Ceci and I went to Paris, Spain, and Switzerland. I flew on all the airlines in Europe, but I didn't enjoy the tour because the guides didn't speak Spanish and I didn't understand a thing. On the second trip, Ceci and I went to Spain. We began the tour in Madrid and then traveled all over Spain until we arrived in beautiful San Sebastián. I loved Spain, really loved it! Then we went to Switzerland, where it was still winter. I always thought that the postcards of trees covered in snow were just fantasy. But there I saw that it was real. Those trees covered with snow were white, white, white, and so beautiful.

After my children married, my sister Delfia came to share the apartment with me. My son Jorge had married a girl in San Cristóbal, and after he settled there he told me, "I don't want you to live in Mexico City any longer. It's very dangerous for two women to be living there alone. Sell your apartment for a low price, but get cash!" So I put an announcement outside the building, and the man who lived in front bought the apartment right away. Jorge sent a moving van, and that's how I returned to San Cristóbal after thirty-five years.

My sister Amada never married and had been living by herself in our family's big house on General Utrilla Street. Now she was sick, and I came to look after her. We got along very well. But it was strange to come home after so many years. I didn't know the people in town anymore, and I had to readjust. I began to have a nervous breakdown because my sister and I were all alone in that enormous old house.

We were there when the Chichonal volcano erupted. There were huge mounds of ashes everywhere, and we were afraid the roof would collapse under the weight. With so much ash in the air, it was dark even during the daytime. Amada and I hid in one little room of the house where my father had his office, and there we locked ourselves in. I made pitchers of *atole*, and that's what we ate. It was a terrible experience.

I stayed with Amada until she died, and then I came to live with Jorge and his family. My daughter Ceci lives next door. I'm now eighty-seven years old and the only one of my ten brothers and sisters still alive.

It's a good thing I've always liked books. My brother Rodolfo was a voracious reader and had a huge library. When my children were small and I was working, I didn't have time for reading. But as I grew older I began to devour books again. Fortunately, I can still see well and sometimes I read all night. Reading keeps me from feeling so lonely.

I almost never leave the house. Sometimes I would like to, but when the weather turns ugly, I'm afraid to go out in the wind.

Now I feel like I'm having another nervous breakdown, and it makes me ashamed in front of my family. I take valerian to calm my nerves. Because I feel so lonesome sometimes, I call for my daughter—"Ceci, Ceci!"—so that she'll come and stay with me.

I'm very Catholic, and I ask God to save me from a long illness. We'll see what he says. I'm praying for an attack that will be quick and painless for me and my children. I'm just waiting for God to come for me. Waiting for the end, that's all.

María Meza Girón

María Meza Girón

My family lived up in the mountains about an hour's walk from Tenejapa. I was born there around sixty-three years ago.

My father died when my little brother was just eight days old. My sister and I were still very little then, so I don't remember my father at all.

My family was very poor. We didn't even have our own cornfield. And our lives were even harder after my father died. We didn't have money or land or even food to eat. My mother worked in other families' cornfields, but the pay was very low. Since I was the oldest child, I stayed home to take care of my little brother and sister. When my mother worked, we were left alone at home. My brother died of measles when he was ten years old.

When I was young, the custom in Tenejapa was for a man and a woman to live together. Rarely did they get married in the church. When I was around fifteen years old I got together like that with a man. Now I don't even remember his name. He's the father of my only son, Pedro. The man and I lived together for about a year, but the relationship wasn't good at all. He had another woman and, besides, he drank a lot of *posh*.

After him, I didn't look for another man. Pedro and I lived with my mother and my sister. Later my cousin, who had left her husband, came to live with us too. My cousin said to me, "Don't look for a man. We'll all take care of Pedro ourselves. Another man won't love your baby. He'll mistreat him because Pedro's not his."

So my son was brought up by a houseful of women. When he was young, we were so poor that we dressed him in rags. Poor Pedro! *Muyuk taquin*—no money!

Life was hard. I had nothing to give my son, sometimes not even food. I worked in the cornfields alongside my mother. The good thing was that all of the women in the family took turns staying at home to look after my son.

When Pedro started school, he had to walk a long, long way to his classes. Many dogs lived on the road, and one of them always terrified him. One day the dog became so ferocious that Pedro ran back home instead of going on to school. Soon the principal came to our house to see why Pedro had missed classes. The principal insisted that I pay a two-peso fine. But I didn't have two pesos! So I had to work extra hours in the cornfield just to earn the money. Those were very, very hard times.

My cousin, who was a very good weaver, taught me how. I watched her and began to make small pieces. They turned out well, and little by little I began to make very nice weavings. My work is good.

One day, in the 1970s, some people who worked for the government came to Tenejapa to buy weavings. I sold them some of my pieces, and for the first time I had a little money.

All of a sudden, many people became interested in my weavings. When Pedro saw all of the interest in my work, he began to make drawings of the designs I weave. No one had ever done that before. The weavers had always just kept the patterns in their heads.

Later, when Chip Morris came to investigate the meanings of our designs, he saw Pedro's drawings. Soon Pedro was drawing our weaving designs for books. When Chip organized the Sna Jolobil store in San Cristóbal, Pedro began to work for them. Later he became the director of the cooperative.

My life has been much better since Pedro started working at Sna Jolobil. I began to sell my weavings there, and Pedro helped me build this nice house. Everything has changed for the better. Now I have my own cornfield and my own house. I have everything I need.

I'm glad that I only had one son. My life would have been much harder if I had more children. Besides, I have a good son. We get along well, and he comes to visit me often. The only problem is that he hasn't married yet. I sometimes wonder if he will ever marry. I'd really like that.

Now I live here in my house with four other women. We're all related, and we all work with Sna Jolobil. The five of us get along well, and we never argue.

None of us is married, and if one gets sick, the others care for her. It's nice living like that.

The only bad thing is that when I was younger my weavings sold better because there weren't so many weavers back then. Now there are many women who weave, and there is more competition. That makes it harder for each woman to sell her own work. The weavers used to be more united. Now there are many groups of weavers and many divisions among them.

I don't weave so much anymore. After working for so many hours, my bones ache, especially in my legs. I get tired much more quickly than before.

Every morning I get up at six o'clock and make my coffee, my tortillas, and then have breakfast. Afterwards, I decide if I'm going to work in my cornfield. It's far away, and I have to walk a long way to get there. If I leave at eight o'clock in the morning, I return home around four in the afternoon. Then the other women in the house and I eat together. I'm doing well. I'm happy. San Ildefonso, our patron saint, has finally answered all my prayers.

Dolores Maceiras, viuda de Suárez

Dolores Maceiras, viuda de Suárez

My parents came from Spain at the beginning of the last century. They left Spain because, you see, conditions were more favorable here in Mexico. First they lived in Tuxtla Gutiérrez, then moved to San Cristóbal where my father opened a store. I was born in 1915, just after my family settled here. Soon after that, the Revolution came to Chiapas.

I had two brothers and three sisters. My sisters played together but never wanted to play with me. They just ignored me. When they'd go to the market, I would eat all their food, and on their return, there'd be nothing left. That was my way of getting back at them. I was always headstrong.

At home my father used to speak to us in Gaelic. When there was someone around whom my mother didn't like, she'd talk to us in Gaelic too. I understood what they said but spoke very little. Gaelic is a pretty language, but how easily one forgets such things.

When I was twelve years old I became the cook in the house. Even though we had servants, my mother wanted us to learn to do things for ourselves. My mother was a very good cook. My aunt Pilar, who owned the Español Hotel, was a good cook too and always asked me to help her in the kitchen. I would watch her make marmalades, and I loved it. Oh, yes, I've always liked to cook.

We all went to the Steinpres School, which was run by Germans. Those Germans were very good teachers. I used to get up at six o'clock in the morning in order to arrive early. I would walk to school and wait until they opened. Can you imagine? I got the best grades in handcrafts. I embroidered around fifty tablecloths when I was in school.

The Steinpreses were nice people. A few years ago my son Gabriel ran into old Mrs. Steinpres, and she gave him a notebook that had belonged to my sister Gene. Mrs. Steinpres had kept it for more than seventy years. Gene is my only sister who's still alive, the only one I have left.

I didn't like Mrs. Steinpres's brother, who was always spying on us. If I made a mistake, it was a sin. I was very mischievous and would pinch people and things like that. So, as punishment, he'd make me walk around the school-yard on my knees.

My mother was just as strict, let me tell you. She wouldn't let us read love stories written by a certain Spanish writer. Mother would lift up the mattress, where she knew we hid the books, and then take them away. We never had the chance to finish them. No, my mother didn't like us to read those kinds of stories.

And every time we went out, she would check to see if we came home on time. If we were a half hour late, she'd punish us. When we arrived late, Gene would go in first. Instead, I would climb the big tree in our patio, thinking that I wouldn't get into trouble. But, no, I couldn't escape my punishment. Sooner or later I had to come down. I couldn't sleep up there in the tree! So I'd climb down, knowing that in the morning it would be my turn for a spanking. I'd lie on some pillows, and my mother would hit me. It didn't hurt much, but I'd cry as if it hurt a lot. My father never hit us. But when my mother told us something and we didn't do it ... well, you can imagine. Yes, my mother was the strong one and my father was the sweet one.

Every day my father would go off to work in his store. And every day at six o'clock in the afternoon, I'd bring him his cake and coffee. That would make him happy. He sold a little bit of everything: fabrics, office supplies, and Tomás Barro shoes that he brought from Mexico City. I loved to look at all the merchandise. He had big storerooms in which he piled bundles of everything. I would climb up on the bundles and then jump off. My sister Gene was always afraid to play those games, but I liked them.

When my father went to Tuxtla to buy goods for the store, he had to go on horseback. In those days, horses or mules carried everything up and down the mountain, because the road was too narrow for a wagon. But I was carried on the back of a Chamula Indian! He would put a cushion on his shoulders, then a chair on top of that, and I would go riding in the chair. They would tie us in, so we wouldn't fall out. Along the way the men would drink *pozol* to give them strength. And don't think they were going slowly. No. They trotted! Just imagine. All that way from San Cristóbal to Tuxtla. The precipices on the side of the trail were terribly steep, and when we passed by, I'd close my eyes. We didn't return in one day, of course. We would stay overnight in Tuxtla while the men rested, and then they would carry us back up the mountain. They carried adults too. It was very impressive. I'm telling you this because I experienced it and know that it's true.

We also went on outings to Ocosingo and Comitán. There's a saying, "Comitán of the flowers, San Cristóbal of the lovers."

My first boyfriend was Maruca Navarro's brother. We went to the movies together at the Zebadua Theater, but we didn't do anything but make eyes at each other. He wouldn't have dared to do anything else. It wasn't like it is today, right? He was very handsome, that boy, very handsome. And then the accident happened. He was killed when he went to visit a girl at La Enseñanza School. The night watchman shot him. That's the way it goes. But by then I was living in Mexico City.

We moved to Mexico City when I was fifteen years old and had finished school. My father started a business making hams and sausages. We had a big house, and we hung the hams out on the roof to dry before we salted them. I was the one in charge of that. I quickly forgot about San Cristóbal.

One day I met my future husband, Valeriano, at the grocery store where we went shopping. He worked at a cement company called Eureka. He always paid attention to me, but I didn't like him because I always saw him playing cards at the store. One evening I went to a party at the Asturiano Center, and he was there. That night he proposed to me and to my two sisters—all three! I thought that was really funny.

When we got home we talked about it. "Look, Mother, Valeriano has proposed to us. He asked me—and her, and her too—on the same day, at the same party!" First he asked one of us to dance, then the other, then the other. Can you believe it? He must have thought, "Let's see if one of them accepts." I told my sisters, "You know what? Let's not pay any attention to him." And so we all turned him down. But we would still see him when we'd have to go to the store. Little by little he started liking me best.

I think I finally decided to marry Valeriano just to see the reaction of my sisters. My parents told me, "Whatever you decide is all right with us. He's a good boy."

We dated for a year, but a chaperone was always with us. So there we were with my mother looking on. How mad that made me! And when we went for walks in the countryside, my mother went too. I still have a photo of all of us, mother sitting there with Gene and her boyfriend and Valeriano and me. We were never alone, never. We could just give little kisses through the garden gate. With so many chaperones, it was impossible to do very much, not even steal a real kiss.

After a year we were ready to be married. I was sixteen and he was twenty-eight. Just imagine, I already knew everything about keeping house. But I really wasn't anxious to leave my parents' home. On our honeymoon we went to Cuernavaca and stayed at the Hotel Casino de la Selva, which was beautiful back then. It had a Mexican wing and a Spanish wing. There we met some friends who had gotten married on the same day. We spent ten days in Cuernavaca and then returned home.

We lived in a small house near my parents but later moved to a bigger place when we started having children. Lolina was born first, and that was one of the happiest times of my life. I thought, "Look how pretty she is. How can it be possible that I gave birth to this beautiful creature!" It really was a miracle. Children make you so happy.

My second daughter, Minita, died at six years of age, because of a problem with her heart. She quit eating, and so we took her to a doctor, who gave her injections. If those injections accelerated her death, we'll never know. She was the first child who died on me. She was a good girl who loved her father very much. But it was God's will.

After that, I had one right after another.

The first time we went to Spain, the airplane wasn't full, so it wasn't so bad traveling with all the family. On the contrary, I even invited a niece to go along with us. But the hotels in New York weren't happy about accepting so many children. Fortunately, Valeriano had a friend in New York who was an ambassador. He was very helpful, but his wife was impatient with the youngsters. She said she couldn't eat with so many kids around. So we took turns. Valeriano ate with the ambassador's wife, and later I ate with the children. We didn't stay long in New York and soon were on the plane to Madrid.

We went to Asturias where I met Valeriano's family. I got along well with my in-laws. Valeriano's father was a gentle person, but his mother had a stronger character, very much like my parents. At first we stayed with them, but then my husband bought a house in Puerto de Vega and we all went there to live. It was a nice house with a beautiful view of the ocean. My son Roberto was born a year and a half later. When we finally returned to Mexico, I was pregnant with Gabriel.

After the war we went back to Spain on vacation. Valeriano had bought a car, a big Cadillac, which he shipped from Veracruz to Lisbon. We picked up the car in Lisbon and then drove through all the Spanish provinces.

In 1947 Evita Perón was the Argentine ambassador to Spain. When we were driving through Barcelona, we saw huge crowds in the streets, waiting for someone. When the people saw our Cadillac they thought that Evita was inside, and they threw themselves at our car. They thought I was Evita Perón! She and I were more or less the same age, and we were both blonde and thin. We looked a lot alike, yes, but I wasn't Evita Perón.

Who would have dreamed that I would have fourteen children! You can't imagine how it was to have so many kids. We had a two-story house, and while my husband and I sat quietly downstairs, visiting with guests, the children were upstairs, getting into trouble. The things they would invent. And the pranks! Once Roberto threw a cat out the window to see if it really had nine lives! "Oh, they're just being kids," Valeriano would say. But sometimes I just couldn't handle it. The children would run from me and I couldn't catch them. I was simply overwhelmed. But in the end, with all their pranks, all my children turned out well.

My marriage was just like I imagined it would be. I had many suitors when I was young, but I always said, "No, I'm going to marry a man I love—a man from Spain." And when I met Valeriano I said, "I found one!" Valeriano's brother, who worked with him, would tell me, "Marry him!" And I did the right thing.

But I'm not going to tell you that he was a saint. The most difficult thing was that he drank. Not at first, though. He didn't start until he began working in the government and had business dinners and obligations. I didn't like his drinking at all, and I'd get very angry with him. There even came a time when I said, "I can't take it anymore." Frankly, it did cross my mind to leave him. But it was impossible to leave when I had so many children. And back then, it was different. Husbands wouldn't let you go even if you wanted to. The only thing I knew how to do was to cook and to sew. I really couldn't do anything else. I had to accept it.

As for the rest, I never lacked for anything, thank God. He just had that one defect. Valeriano was a very dutiful man and a good person. Every time I gave birth he was there with me. He was always very attentive, and there were many good times with him.

We went to lots of parties. Valeriano loved to sing and dance the flamenco. He would bring home the singers of that era, and once Lola Flores came to the house and sang and danced. When Valeriano called out my name, "Lola!" I would have to come down and feed all the guests. I always had sausages prepared and anything else they might want. But if I didn't—why do I even tell you this!

He loved it when the princesses were chosen for the Asturiano Center. In fact, several of our daughters were chosen as princesses. Valeriano would invite everybody to eat and celebrate. I went everywhere with him, to dances and formal parties. I still have many of my evening dresses, and what dresses they were! One beautiful gown was all lace. I gave another one to my daughter Tere, who's a film producer, but I don't know if she still has it or if she used it in one of her movies. That was a wonderful time of my life, and I enjoyed it all with Valeriano.

But things changed when Valeriano became ill. He didn't have the same spirit as before. He developed a stomach ulcer and was very sick. He was in the hospital for just two weeks, and then they sent him home. Perhaps he could have lived for a few more years, but he didn't. It helped me a lot that he accepted his death so calmly. He died fully aware of what was happening to him, so somehow it wasn't so bad. I was able to say good-bye to him, which was important. I kissed him good-bye, but, yes, I was very sad when he died.

If I could live my life over, there are things I would do differently. I would have liked to study more. People always told me, "With everything you know about cooking, you should give classes." But I would say to myself, "How can I give classes with so many children to look after?" When I was still single and living in Mexico City I went to a cooking academy. But later my life was filled with family.

Sometimes I think, "My God, I haven't done anything in my life. I'll pass on without leaving anything. I really should have done more." Sometimes I'm very dissatisfied with myself. What good are all these books I have when I don't know how to put them to good use? My family said to me, "It's incredible. With everything you know, you've gotten into a rut. You haven't done anything lately. We'll help you write a cookbook."

Just recently, my daughter Marta told me, "Let's do it!"

So I said to her, "Go ahead. You start. You're the one with a computer."

If we do the cookbook, it will make me very happy. I'll see if I can really do it!

Victoria Aguilar Hernández

Victoria Aguilar Hernández

The day before yesterday I was sprawled out on the floor, sick with a terrible cough. I felt so bad that I couldn't do a thing. When I get a cough like that, my heart starts beating fast. When that happens, I drink *horchata* mixed with fennel and Alka-Seltzer. Today I felt so much better that I even went out to gather my firewood.

I don't know how old I am because my parents never told me what day I was born on, here in Aguacatenango. Some people say I'm around seventy years old.

My parents worked in San Cristóbal until my father left my mother for another woman. When I was little I didn't want to go to work cleaning houses with my mother. I cried so much that my poor mother couldn't get anything done. So my grandmother took me back to live with her in Aguacatenango. She's the one who brought me up. My grandmother was a very good woman.

When I was ten years old I learned how to make tortillas. At first I made just tiny ones. My grandmother showed me how to form the *masa* into little balls and then how to flatten them out into tortillas. Back then, we didn't have a press to flatten the tortillas. We had to do it by hand. Tortillas made by hand taste much better, and when I cook them on the *comal*, they puff up so pretty.

I was never married, but I lived with the father of my three children. My husband, Juan Rodriguez, was one of the best things in my life. I met him at school, where I went for a while to learn to read and write a little. That's where Juan and I fell in love. He was young and thin and kind. I never had anything but good times with him. I always had my corn and beans. And I always felt loved.

One day Juan said to me, "It hasn't started raining, so I can't plant my corn yet. I'm going to see if I can find work at the sugar refinery in Pujiltic. Then I'll come back to plant our cornfield."

"All right," I said. "I'll make some cakes and some sandwiches for you to take along."

"Make me enough for three days," he told me. "And maybe a little more in case I find work."

We were very poor and didn't have enough money to buy a bus ticket to Pujiltic. But a truck was leaving before daybreak to carry men to the refinery. Before he left that morning, my husband said, "I'm going now. Promise me that you won't scold the children while I'm gone." Then he left. Later that day I heard an announcement on the radio. "The men who left from Aguacatenango this morning to work in Pujiltic have had an accident!"

That's how my husband died. He came back to me in a box.

Juan had been a good husband. If he drank, it was just for one day, and the next day he would go to work. He never drank for two or three days in a row. And he never yelled at me or hit me. I was never afraid of him.

After Juan was gone, my life was sad. I was left all alone with my three little children. I still miss him to this day.

Other men came looking for me, but I wasn't interested. They say that if the first husband was good, the second will be bad. I believe that. So I told those other men, "Excuse me, I'm better off alone."

I lived with my mother and my sisters-in-law, but our children fought a lot and I decided it would be better for me to leave. So I went to San Cristóbal to work as a servant for a while. My mother stayed in Aguacatenango to look after my children. That's how I was able to eat and buy food for my family.

Around that time one of my sisters-in-law was pregnant with her first child. When the baby was about to be born, her midwife was up in the mountains gathering firewood. I was at home, sick in bed, listening to what was happening in the house. My mother kept shouting, "She's going to die! My daughter-in-law is going to die!" The midwife was nowhere to be found. My mother was so scared. Neither she nor my sister-in-law was very brave. And I was so sick!

I thought, "Dear God, what am I going to do? Is what my mother says true? Is my sister-in-law going to die? Should I do something? Or should I just keep lying here in bed and let her die?" I finally decided, "I'm going to see if I can help." So I got out of bed and tied back my hair.

"Mother, what is going on?" I asked.

"Oh, daughter," my mother moaned, "the midwife's not coming."

I went to my sister-in-law and asked, "What's wrong with you?"

She cried, "I think I'm going to die!"

"Where's the medicine the midwife brought to you? Mama, bring it here!"

"Are you going to help your sister-in-law?" my mother asked, looking very surprised.

"Yes," I told her. "I'm going to do her a favor."

"That's wonderful," said my mother. "She's not going to die, then."

We prepared the herbs to make a tea and gave it to my sister-in-law. Next I rubbed herbs on her stomach. All along I kept asking myself, "Where did I learn this? How do I know the right thing to do?" No one had ever taught me any of this. Somehow I knew in that moment exactly what to do. The baby was born healthy. No one had taught me to cut the umbilical cord, but I knew just how to do it. I figured it out all by myself.

I don't remember if I ever dreamed about being a midwife before that day. But, you know, your dreams can guide you and tell you what to do. Sometimes when I wake up from my dreams I take a few branches from the orange tree that grows in my yard and I hold them in my arms. I've done that since I was very little, and it has always helped me. I was sick a lot when I was young. My stomach hurt, and my face would swell up. My poor parents spent so much money on medicine for me. But when I began to take the orange branches in my arms after waking from a dream, I started to get well and not fall sick so often. A healer also gave me an amulet of flowers and ribbons. That seems to help too.

When a baby is born here in Aguacatenango, people have a custom of giving gifts of *atole*, sweet breads, and cocoa beans to the family. Since people here don't have enough money to buy chocolate in the stores, we grind cocoa beans on a stone. Then we mix it with water and make a chocolate drink to celebrate the arrival of the newborn baby. Three days after the birth, we kill a chicken and prepare a meal. That's the custom here.

After my sister-in-law's baby was born, my aunt came to bring the *atole*. We began to talk, and she asked me, "Who helped with the birth?"

My mother told her, "Look, we couldn't find the midwife, and suddenly Victoria got out of bed and helped us deliver the baby."

"Oh, that's good," my aunt said. "From now on we won't have to look somewhere else for a midwife."

So that's how I began my work. Little by little, women came to look for me. Soon other midwives came to visit me, and even doctors from other countries came to learn from me. I've been a midwife for years, and I'm still working today.

I don't remember how many babies I've brought into the world. I've never counted them. But the first children I delivered have had children with me, and soon they will have their own babies.

I buy some of the herbs I use during the births in Villa las Rosas. Others I gather from the countryside. I use them to ease the pain and to help hurry along the birth. Afterwards, I bind the mother's stomach. She rests the next day, and on the third day I give her a steam bath with herbs.

It can be very dangerous if the placenta doesn't come out after the baby. A friend of mine had her baby at eight o'clock in the morning. I don't know if her midwife gave her medicine. But the placenta didn't come out until three o'clock in the afternoon, after the midwife had already gone home. My friend was lucky that she didn't die.

If the placenta doesn't come out by itself, the midwife has to put her hand inside the mother to pull it out. But it can't be done just any way. The hands have to be very clean and the fingernails cut short. Then the hands must be covered in cooking oil.

Two weeks ago a woman was having her baby, and because the midwife couldn't attend to her, the family came to look for me. The baby was born just fine, but I had to take out the placenta. Since I saved the mother's life, I thought, "Maybe they'll pay me a little more money." But no, they didn't give me anything extra.

I don't charge for my work. I just receive whatever people want to give me—one hundred pesos, a little coffee, or a little sugar. I don't have much. We're poor. My children help me out a little, but even with that, it's sometimes not enough to live on. A doctor in San Cristóbal tells me, "Charge a fee after the birth. Make sure the family brings you some rice too." It would be very nice if people would at least pay me with a little coffee, sugar, or rice.

Just once in all these years has one of my mothers died giving birth. If I see that it's going to be a difficult labor, I carry the woman to the hospital, especially if I see that there might be complications. The mother who died was very overweight. She seemed fine each time I went to check on her. The baby was in the correct position. At three o'clock in the morning, her family came to wake me up. By noon the next day a healthy baby boy was born. The mother didn't bleed too much. But when I placed the baby on her chest for her to hold for the first time, the mother's eyes rolled back in her head and she died. I never knew why. Only God knows.

The mother's family was very upset with me. They even threatened to kill me. So I went to the medical office in Amatenango to explain what happened. I thought, "Well, if they're going to kill me, then just let them!" But the doctor told me, "Don't worry." He assured me that sometimes, even with doctors, a mother or a baby will die during birth. So the family didn't kill me. In fact, nothing bad happened. The mother's family stopped talking to me for a while, but now we're speaking again.

I've never lost a baby. There are times when the umbilical cord gets wrapped around the baby's neck—sometimes two or even three times. When that happens, I have to cut the cord right away so that the baby doesn't die.

Sometimes the baby comes standing up, instead of headfirst. I remember one mother whose baby was coming like that. The other midwives, who were *espiritistas*, told the family that the baby would not live. During the birth, the healers got scared, and that night the mother's family came to look for me. But I told them, "I can't help you. I'm afraid that the *espiritistas* who are attending the mother will become envious and will practice witchcraft on me. Or if something goes wrong, you'll take it out on me!"

The family told me that I shouldn't worry, that no one would harm me. So I went with them to see about the birth. It seems that the mother had already been in labor for three days, but I wasn't afraid. The baby was positioned feet first. But I just turned him around inside the womb. After I did that, both mother and baby were fine.

Nowadays there are many midwives in Aguacatenango, so I don't attend as many births as I used to. When I first started, there were just three midwives. All of us are still birthing babies. But there are also many *espiritista* midwives, and like I said before, we don't get along very well. There's a lot of competition among us and lots of envy. The *espiritistas* get angry with us and don't speak to us. That creates a problem in a town so small. If the family comes to talk to me, I will do them the favor of attending to the mother. If not, I don't get involved.

My work has been a wonderful and important part of my life. Two weeks ago I attended two births, and in July and August I will bring two more babies into the world. I'm not a nurse. I'm not an *espiritista* or a healer. I'm a midwife who works all by myself.

Koh María (and Koh)

Koh María

Koh María is my name. Just Koh María—no last name. I don't know how old I am. I was born in Nahá, on the other side of the lake. I had three mothers and many brothers and sisters. My real mother was born in Nahá but moved to Lacanjá when she began to have problems here. I think someone was beating her, so she left. I was very little when my mother went away. I loved her very much. Now she's very old and doesn't hear or see so well anymore.

I was twelve years old when I married Chan K'in Viejo. He already had a wife. Her name was Koh. I got along well with her. There used to be another wife—the first one—but she died very young. A snake bit her. So after she died, Chan K'in came to look for me. I was forced to marry him. My mother advised me, "It's better that he has another wife so she can cook your food, so she can grind the corn and make your tortillas."

Girls are always forced to marry the men. You're always told, "Go get married so that you can prepare the man his food." My husband thought that women were here to make his food and to wash his clothes and to have his children.

I didn't like Chan K'in in the beginning. No. He was always trying to put his arms around me, always trying to hug me, and I didn't want him to. I kept pushing him away. I was very afraid of my husband. I didn't want to be close to him, so we slept apart. When we first started living together, he would hit me. But later, not so much. After two or three months I got used to him. Yes, I fell in love with him.

I had ten children, four girls and six boys. When I had my first child I was very happy. It didn't hurt. I gave birth all by myself, without any medicine. Chan K'in's older wife, Koh, helped deliver the baby. She took care of me. Just one of my babies died. He was very, very tiny.

We didn't have a clinic, and we didn't have medicine. But I wasn't at all afraid. My husband would go to the temple to pray to the gods. He called to Hächäkyum to help me. And, yes, it worked, both for me and for his other wives.

When Chan K'in's new wife came to live with us, my children were already big. At first I was a little jealous, but now we love each other. When she married my husband she was very, very young, around eight or nine years old. She tells me that she doesn't remember any of it. She thought I was her other mother. I took care of her as if she were my daughter, but she was really my husband's wife. I raised her and looked after her as if she were my child.

There was nothing but jungle then. There were jaguars, monkeys, wild boar, deer, pheasant, and armadillo. Monkey was really tasty. We ate his little arms. Or we'd put a pheasant in the fire to cook with corn. But what I most liked to eat was wild boar. Really, really delicious!

We used to grow tobacco. The tobacco grew big and healthy, and there was lots of it. But now the leaves are tiny. The plants die because the soil is not as rich as it used to be. That's why the tobacco doesn't grow.

We didn't have many clothes before. We made everything by hand. We wove our husband's tunics out of cotton that we grew ourselves. We colored the cotton with dye that we made from the leaves and skin of certain trees. We'd add a little lime and make a bright yellow color. Have you seen the clothes in the museum at Na Bolom? I was the one who made them when Trudi Blom was still alive.

When Trudi came to visit us, she used to bring us blankets, because we didn't have anything to cover us at night. Before that, we just slept in our clothes, and it was cold.

When I first met Trudi, she was young and pretty and still single. Her boyfriend had left her, but she found another one. Later they were married. Her husband, Pancho, was a very nice man, the perfect man in her life.

I used to be very happy. But then two of my children died, one girl and one boy. After they were gone, everything turned sad in this house. I want to tell you what happened.

My daughter Nuk was very young when Leo came. She was just eight years old. Leo came from America with Roberto Bruce, the anthropologist. Leo was Roberto's nephew. Nuk started going to Leo's house to ask for food, like the children always did. Then one day Leo came to ask my husband for permission to marry her.

Chan K'in forced Nuk to marry Roberto's nephew. My husband didn't even talk to me about it. Koh and I didn't know what was happening. Chan K'in said, "Women are supposed to get married, not to live for many years in their father's house."

I cried, "Please, no!" I was very upset when she married Leo.

Leo was crazy. He stole things. Leo even sent my daughter out to steal. My daughter didn't want to steal things from people. But he would say to her, "Go steal or you'll die right now."

Leo didn't stay with Nuk in their house. He slept in some other place and left her alone in the house at night. And when he'd come home, he'd hit my daughter. He slapped her and whipped her. He mistreated my daughter. I saw him do it.

The first few times he beat her, Nuk escaped to my daughter-in-law's house. She said, "Help me. Leo's going to kill me!"

Leo drank a lot. One night he got drunk and screamed all night long. He was acting crazy. They had a fight. He hit her, and Nuk fell down the steps. She broke her jaw.

Some neighbors ran to tell me, "Please come to help your daughter! Her husband's going to kill her!" They said that Leo was kicking her. It was as if she wasn't even a person. He hit her and kicked her as if she were an animal. But nobody hid her from him. And he killed her.

We're still very afraid of him. They say that Leo is nearby in Palenque. They say that he shaved his head and wears dark glasses so that we can't see who he is.

The other very sad thing in my life was when my son Chan K'in Quinto died. He was murdered too. When dawn came, my grandson found him dead. He came to me and said, "Grandmother, my uncle is dead. Come see! I saw him, and he's very cold."

"No! No!" I said. "I don't believe it. You must be joking." So we went to see. My son was lying face down, and he was all purple. I couldn't see him well because there was so much blood. I said, "He's already dead. We should-n't move him. If you move him, people are going to accuse you. They're going to say that you killed him."

The truth is, I don't know who killed my son. He was very young when he died. He was a good son. He worked hard.

Now my husband is dead. Two of my children are dead. Chan K'in Quinto was killed. My daughter Nuk was killed. Why did I lose my children? Why me?

Then there's my son El Mudo, the one who can't speak. He's living in Monte Líbano. He left because he couldn't find a wife here in Nahá. They say that he drinks a lot. One day he sent me greetings and a photo to remember him by. He told me not to forget him. He sent us a hug. But he doesn't want to come back. He's gone, then. My son's going to die in Monte Líbano.

When my husband, Chan K'in Viejo, died, my heart was broken inside. We couldn't even eat. And when my son Quinto and my daughter Nuk died, it was the same. Now I'm a little happier because all those sad times are over. I don't think about it so much anymore.

You see, since our husband died, Koh and I have changed our religion. What do you think about us leaving our gods? I want to explain to you why. We can't take care of our gods. We can't make a ceremony or pray. It's against our customs. The true Hächäkyum said, "Women can't go into the god house. They can't touch the god pots." Women could only make the tortillas for the gods. We made *atole*, *pozol*, and tamales. We cooked in the women's kitchen while the men were praying in the god house.

The god house is still near our house, but we don't go there anymore. Now we go to the Baptist church, but only on Sunday. Saturday, no. Just Sunday!

The preacher came and sat down right here and talked to us. We felt bad because we didn't want to change our religion. I said, "We don't want to change."

But the preacher said, "If you join us, if you believe in our god, when you die you're going to see Chan K'in Viejo up in heaven. You'll find your husband again. You'll see him there in paradise."

The pastor spoke very well. So now we're Baptists.

But I think my husband's ceremonies were much nicer.

Herminia Haro Haro

Herminia Haro Haro

My whole life changed in a very profound way when I came to Chiapas to live and work. That was more than fifty years ago. At that time the God I believed in was a God who punished and rewarded, a God who was distant, like my father, a God who scared me a little. In Chiapas all that changed. Here I've found a God who is softer, more merciful.

I came into this world on April 3, 1935, on a small ranch in the state of Zacatecas. My father bought and sold pigs for a living. There were seven children in my family. My two sisters and I were close to the same age. We always wished for a brother. Our parents wouldn't let us go out alone, and we thought that with a brother along we might be allowed to leave the house. But when our brothers were finally born, they were too young and didn't want to have anything to do with us.

My parents got along well, even though my father had a strong personality, one that demanded respect. He expected us to work. So we three daughters shared the chores. One of us carried the water, another ground the corn. My oldest sister made the tortillas. My father taught us how to plant corn, how to take care of the fields and to pick the crops. I've always liked to work on the land.

Because my father was often away from home, our mother would allow us to go out to play after we finished our chores. We played in the fields, turning cartwheels in the grass. Or we'd pick flowers and take them to church as offerings for the Virgin of Guadalupe. When I'd see the statue of the Virgin with her crown of flowers, I always thought that those were the flowers I had brought her from our fields.

We made violins and guitars out of corn leaves. We made pots out of clay. Or we'd collect broken pieces of colored glass, mix them with cow dung, and toss them in the fire. The heat would melt the glass into all kinds of shapes that we played with like toys.

Many times we'd be singing and playing when my father came home. Just one look from him and we knew to behave. But when my father came home whistling, we'd know he was in a good mood. My mother would say to us, "Why don't you go outside to play?" Or our father would ask, "Don't you have something to do?" We'd just laugh because we knew exactly why they wanted us out of the house.

I never had any tender moments with my father. He was the authority, and his word was law. We were a little closer to our mother. She often smiled at us. Nowadays parents and children hug each other. But back then, people didn't express their feelings. We had a cousin whose parents treated her with tenderness, but they also hit her a lot. Our parents never hit us, but neither did they show us much affection.

My mother, who is ninety-seven, is an extremely calm and patient woman. My sister-in-law once asked my mother about her life with my father. I discovered that she loved my father from the very beginning, and she learned to adapt to his personality. She said that she never suffered. That may very well be true.

I have the joy and patience of my mother and the strength and stubbornness of my father. Those qualities have helped me in my work and in my life.

When I was young I wanted to serve God, but I didn't know how. "I don't want to be married," I told myself. Perhaps unconsciously I didn't want to live a life like my mother's. But I don't remember consciously thinking that. Yes, there were some exchanges of looks and smiles with boys, but it was just a game, nothing serious. I don't think I've ever been in love.

First my little sister went away to the convent. But later she left it and eventually married. I was the traditional, obedient daughter. When I was sixteen I entered the convent too. I was very happy there. But after a few months my parents wanted me to come home and think about my decision a little more.

I went back to the convent on April 1, 1952. It was a Sunday. My father had said that he would take me, but he was busy with his work. I waited for him anxiously, hoping that he would hurry home. When he finally arrived he took me to the convent by donkey. That was our only means of transportation back then.

My parents were pleased with my decision to become a nun. My father told me, "That way I won't have to argue with a son-in-law." He came to visit me every week. And both my mother and father attended the ceremony when I took my vows. Even though they didn't express their feelings, I could see in their faces that they were happy and proud of me. I was happy too.

When my father was sick and about to die, I was a long way from home, attending an assembly of nuns. My sister said to my father, "Herminia is so far away!" He woke up a little and said, "Let her be. She has her business to do!"

During my early years in the convent, I was never ill. But suddenly I became sick with fevers. I was in my twenties, but I felt like an old lady. I lived closed up inside the convent, doing my chores. So I said to God, "If you don't want me here, then send me where I can work with the people." That's when I was suddenly sent to Chiapas. The other Sisters told me, "Why do you want to go so far away if you're so sick?" But my work with the people here rejuvenated me. First of all, I liked the house in Chilón. It was much more open than the convent I had been living in. I liked the Sisters, and I enjoyed working with a mixed group of Brothers and Jesuit priests.

During those first years, we walked everywhere through the jungle. We walked hours and hours, days and days. Once a Sister who was with me suddenly shouted, "Herminia, look! A snake!" Then a little while later, "Look, another snake!" We wore green boots, and the snakes were the same color as our boots. Father Mardonio, who was traveling with us, said, "Better have the guide go in front with his machete."

Many times when we were with Father Mardonio he would call out to us, "Just look at that flower! And that flower!" But sometimes Father Mardonio would become exasperated with us because we stopped so often.

Once another Sister and I were in such a hurry to reach a community that we forgot to bring our blankets. It was night, and it was raining. And there was no electricity in that isolated place. We covered ourselves with plastic and slept sitting on a bench. Under the plastic, with the rain, cold, and humidity of the jungle, we were really sweating. My companion told me, "If I don't get tuberculosis now, I never will!" Back then, there was a lot of tuberculosis in Chiapas. But that didn't scare me, and I was never infected.

When the roads were built, we could walk in the dark, so we began to travel at night. Many times the other nuns and I would travel alone. We would arrive at a village, and people would invite us to stay. It was so safe and peaceful, and the villagers were very respectful. They looked after us and loved us. When we finally stopped for the night in a community, they always gave us a place to sleep on the floor.

When we began working in Chilón, the jungle was unspoiled. There was no running water or electricity. It was totally uncivilized. You could hear the howler monkeys roaring in the trees. I've watched the jungle disappear over the years, and now it's dying. It looks so sad. The communities have been growing, and people haven't found a way to live in harmony with nature.

Now we have paved roads and travel to the communities by car. When civilization arrived, other things began to change. Now there are drugs like marijuana. There's the paramilitary and a lot of people with guns. Many people have been killed in this area. You never know what's going to happen next. All this started just before the Zapatista Uprising in 1994.

I'm not an intellectual. I don't know much, but I did learn to read and write. When I first came to Chiapas I went to the indigenous communities to give courses in catechism. Someone always came with me to translate. But I didn't like that. So I had them write down my course in Tzeltal Maya and I memorized the words. That way I could go without a translator. At first the people laughed at me. But I like humble, simple people. I enjoyed talking to them so much that I finally learned their language, even though I still don't speak it perfectly.

While walking everywhere and talking with people, I saw their living conditions, I saw their suffering. The Tzeltal Indians are special, and I've grown to love them. It impresses me that they share what they have even though they're so poor. I've seen very difficult family situations: men who drink, men who beat their wives. It seems that women suffer more. We women are different. We're more tender. Men are harder and tougher. I've tried to understand why men drink so much, but I've never been able to figure it out.

I've seen that the lives of some indigenous women have improved because of the Zapatista Movement. The Zapatistas say they want to give women a better place in indigenous societies. The idea that women are just as important as men has changed the consciousness of many women. They now know their rights. They listen and they learn. And because of that, there have been improvements. Now women have hope for a change.

Before, women weren't allowed to leave their houses. Now many women leave their homes and even their communities. But I've also seen that this puts them at great risk. Many women go on marches with the men, who really don't give women their proper place even then. Many women just end up coming home pregnant. And then they have problems because the men don't accept responsibility. When the men find out that a child is on the way, they leave the women to fend for themselves. The woman is always the one to pay the price. So even though the Zapatista theory toward women is fine, I don't see that it works in practice.

In many communities there is a huge division among people who are with and people who are against the Zapatistas. No one wants to talk openly about the subject. They are afraid to commit themselves to either side, especially to outsiders. If they're not Zapatistas, they don't want to appear as if they are. And if they really are Zapatistas, they want even less to reveal themselves.

Our most difficult problems come when people with different ideologies in our group begin to clash. Sometimes someone comes to talk to us about the path of revolution. Those ideas have helped us grow. But there is still a great deal of conflict. Because of so many disagreements, people stop speaking to one another. That makes things even more difficult, and then nothing can be resolved.

I haven't had problems with either one side or the other. I've kept my opinions to myself so as not to hurt anybody. That way I can be a bridge between the two. I believe there needs to be another way of doing things. What we need is to come together and ask each other, "What is it that we have in common?" But I know that's hard to do.

There are six Sisters in our congregation in Chilón. And there are eight Sisters in the Tzeltal congregation. Theirs is the only group of purely indigenous nuns in all of Mexico. The group was consecrated by Bishop Samuel Ruiz so that they could maintain their culture, language, and customs. The Younger Sisters of the Divine Shepherd are unique.

In my pastoral work and in the health field, I work with men. But my most important work is with the women's cooperative. They do the traditional cross-stitch embroidery typical of the Tzeltal Indians in this area. Now the women not only embroider their blouses, but also bags, purses, backpacks, and even the vestments for the priests. We encourage them to try different color combinations too. All of this helps them to reach a broader market. This is exclusively women's work, and we are doing very well.

Sometimes we are asked what else we would like to accomplish in our work with the people. I always tell them, "I'll take on whatever comes!"

I want to keep working with a fresh attitude and to act from my heart even more. But at my age I have to be realistic. I simply want to keep being with and serving my people. I don't aspire to anything more. I live and work each day and try not to think too much. Not even about my own death. That doesn't scare me. Every once in a while, when I think about how old I am, I say to myself, "I don't have much more time." I prepare myself for my end by saying, "I will accept this. I've been with the people. I've done what I could." I offer myself to the will of God. That gives me peace. When death does come to me, I ask God to be with me and to carry me to him.

I've been in two accidents. When the first accident happened, I began to pray and immediately became very calm. The other accident happened on a bus on the way to Oaxaca. The bus rolled down a mountain, and eight of my friends were killed. I could hear their screams as the bus was falling. We went down and down, and then everything went dark. It was as if I were falling into a deep well. It was horrible. But I asked God not to abandon me. I told him, "Be with us!" That helped calm me. I grabbed the feet of my companion who was riding in the seat behind me. But when I touched her I realized that she was dead. I had bumps and bruises but nothing serious.

In the critical moments of those two accidents, I felt neither fear nor sadness. Death doesn't frighten me. But, yes, life passes so quickly. The things that I enjoy keep me going. Problems last for a while and then they go away. That's what I've seen.

I like to accompany people in their suffering, but I also enjoy the many parties and festivals we hold in Chilón. When I celebrated my twenty-fifth anniversary with the congregation, people came to sing "Las mañanitas" to me. And when I celebrated my fiftieth anniversary in the congregation I experienced many beautiful moments. On occasions like that, I am really moved by the affection people have shown to me.

Life has taught me to enjoy and to share, to know how to understand different people and their varying opinions. I have learned that each one of us is different. And I've learned to lower my guard and to accept each person as he is.

Mine has been a very good life.

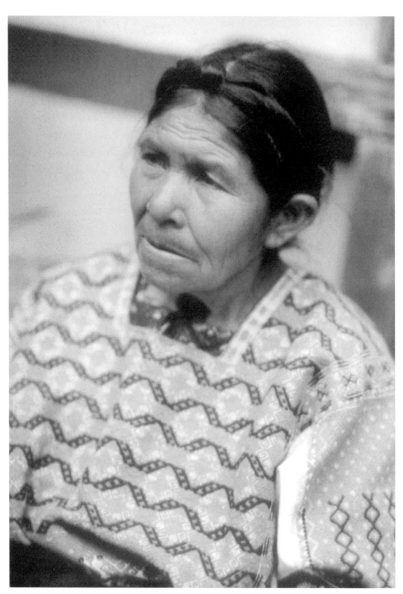

Pascuala Pérez Gómez

Pascuala Pérez Gómez

When my father was walking on this earth, ohhh, he was nothing but a drunk! Once he fasted for three days, eating nothing but a few small tortillas. Then he went into the cave where the Earth Lords live. While he was praying inside the cave, my father saw a vision that announced that a saint would be coming to him. So he bought a box to receive the saint, knowing that it would enter his box. It was a small pine box, cut with an axe.

My father would lean over his box, with a woolen shawl draped over his head, and he would talk to it. Yes, he said that God was inside his box. Of course, no one was ever allowed to look inside the box, but I don't think there was anything inside.

People who were sick from all kinds of illnesses came from all over to talk with the saint who lived inside the box. Supposedly it would cure them. My father's box had the medicine they were looking for. It could heal their souls. A liter of *posh*, three liters of *posh*, and they would begin to pray to the box. "Please, dear God, may I be forgiven. Receive this *posh* as my offering."

So that's how my father became a drunk. My mother too. Both of them took care of the saint in the box. And they were drunk all the time. My mother was even drunk when she made tortillas.

I don't know if any of the sick people who came to our house got well. I just saw them drinking all day and all night. And I was left all alone. Abandoned. That's how I grew up. The others—my parents and their visitors—would take out their machetes and their hatchets and chase after me and my six brothers and sisters. But they never hurt us. We were too fast for them.

There was nothing good in my childhood. No! It was hard because everyone around my house was always drunk. We never went anywhere. We didn't even have clothes. We only ate leaves and beans. And there were many times when we went hungry.

One day my father went out to look for a husband for me. It was just terrible because he came back with an old man! That man was maybe forty years old, and I was around twelve. Back then, I was very pretty and very delicate. And that old man really scared me. Even though I didn't want to be with him, I had to marry him.

For two years I didn't let him touch me. I wouldn't sleep with him. When he came after me each night, I ran from him. My father asked me, "Why don't you give yourself to your husband? You should obey!" he shouted.

Everyone said, "Even though the old man hits her, she still doesn't follow orders!"

But he really never hit me. He just waited. And finally I started sleeping with the old man. But my life didn't get any better because my husband worked with my father and his box. So the old man was drunk all the time too. And I was hungry.

By the time I was fifteen years old I began to take care of myself. I knew how to grind corn and make tortillas. I even drank *posh* sometimes.

Once, when I was about seventeen years old, I went to talk to the saint in the box. I told him, "Please help me, Lord. Help me." That's how I prayed to the box. And it answered me, "Don't let your heart be sad. I'm going to help you." Later I went to the church in San Andrés Larrainzar and prayed to the apostle, the patron saint, there.

Finally I couldn't stand it anymore, and I ran away from my husband. I had given birth to two babies, but they both died. So I was alone.

By then I was twenty and too old to start learning to weave, but I taught myself anyway. I began by looking at the small weavings made by other women. I learned all the different patterns and all the ways of weaving, even brocades. I could just look at a new pattern and know how to weave it. Soon I supported myself by selling my work.

Meanwhile, my parents kept talking to the saint in the box—and kept drinking *posh*. My father's bed was right next to the fire pit, and one night he was so drunk that he fell out of bed, directly into the fire. He burned his chest and his arms so badly that he only lived for three months. During those three months, he kept talking to the saint in the box, asking it for help. But little by little he died. After that, the Christ in the box disappeared. The box stopped talking. So my mother threw it in the trash. No offspring were born to that saint. It just went into the garbage!

After my father died, my mother and all the family became Catholics. We went to church, lit our candles, and listened to the word of God. At church I learned that the saint in the box had been the work of the devil. That was when my mother stopped drinking *posh*.

A few years later my mother got sick, and instead of asking the box to cure her, we prayed that maybe it was better for her to die. After her death, we had a funeral for her, complete with a novena, just like the Catholics do.

When I was twenty-four years old I found another husband. This time I picked him out myself. He was a man my own age. But he turned out to be a mean person too. He promised me skirts and blouses, but the only things he ever gave me were beatings.

I had to do all the work. I got up early every day to grind the corn on the metate. I had to take care of our four cows and twenty sheep. I even had to work in the cornfield. The only thing my husband ever did was tell me what to do. He even told me, "You don't do anything. You're living here for free."

When he sat down to eat and the tortillas weren't immediately on the table, he would throw them at me. If I didn't make the *atole* really fast, he would get furious. Or if the chicken soup wasn't ready the second he wanted it, he would say, "Throw it out to the damn dogs!"

When my husband sold a cow or a chicken, who knows where the money went. I never saw any of it. He controlled everything. He hid all the money in the fields or in other hiding places where I couldn't find it. Then he spent it on beer and *posh*. He even invited all his friends over to drink with him! The only money I ever had was from the sale of the wool from my sheep.

I had seven children with him, five girls and two boys. Each time I gave birth, he wouldn't help me at all. He wouldn't bring me a midwife or even give me *pozol*. I had my children all alone. And every time another girl was born, the man would get madder and madder, because he wanted boys, not girls. Right after each birth I would have to get up to chop the wood to prepare his food.

That man was just a bad seed. So, after thirteen years of living with him, I took my children and left. I had a small cornfield, but that wasn't enough to feed us. Since I knew how to weave, I sold my weavings to be able to buy corn.

Later I found another man—the third. And that man was a good one. He was nice and he was rich, so rich that we could afford to drink coffee! Oh, he was a good man, but he was married. That's why we only lasted two years together.

Meanwhile, my other husband took away my children. I missed them so much that I went back to live near them.

I would have liked to have tried out other men, but I never found one good enough. They're all the same. They just give beatings and more beatings. So I stopped looking. It didn't make sense to look for another man because, you see, I already had my children.

I want to be a good example for them. I don't want them to be like their father. To teach with words doesn't work very well. You have to teach by setting a good example. So I don't drink *posh* anymore. Well, every once in a while, but just one shot, that's all. There aren't any beatings in my children's families. Life is much better for them. It's not the same as when I was growing up. Now there's not so much drinking, and fathers don't choose your husband for you anymore. Instead, parents ask if you want to get married. Nowadays the men even come and bring you gifts of soft drinks! Much better!

I'm seventy years old now. I live with my son near San Andrés Larrainzar, at the foot of Pamalvitz, the sacred Incense Mountain. There are many tall mountains around our house, and when it's cold, they're covered with frost. There are thick green forests, and the trees give me plenty of firewood.

I'm doing well. Nothing breaks my heart. Nothing makes me cry. I plant my garden and I weave. I like to go to San Cristóbal to visit and to walk in the streets. When I was married, my husbands were jealous, and they wouldn't let me leave the house. Those men just caused problems. Now I go shopping with my daughter whenever I want.

Of course, we all will die someday. That's what everyone says: no matter how old you get, you're still going to die in the end. Nothing can be done about that. But I'm not afraid. Why should I be? Well, I was afraid when I ran away from my first husband. I was terrified of him. But I'm not afraid of death.

Anyway, it would be a shame for me to die now. For the last two years I've been working a new plot of land. It belongs to my son, because in San Andrés women can't own land like they can in Chamula.

When I first saw my land I said, "I want to grow pretty flowers and some nice vegetables here. I want to plant my chayote and squash." Yes, it would be a shame to die now. I want to keep planting. I want to keep growing.

Rosa López

Rosa López

You know, I don't even know my real name. Uuuyyy! And God only knows in what year I was born. I really can't tell you. My great-grandson Ivan tells me that I'm 125 years old. But my daughter Rosita says I'm 108. Who knows!

I was born in Chamula. Later I ended up on the ranch of an Indian family, but I don't remember how I got there. There had been a great famine and there was very little food, just a penny's worth of *panela*. This was back when there was no such thing as sugar, just *panela*.

I was looking for something to eat, and at the same time I was looking from one place to another for my parents. But they were nowhere to be found. Yes, I used to have a mother and a father, but I don't remember what happened to them.

I do remember that some Indians gave me a tortilla but without salt. "Do you want to go with us?" they asked.

"Yes, I'll go," I said.

They had a huge blanket, and they set me down on top of it, folded me inside, and threw me over their shoulders. I was about seven years old, not very big at all. I don't remember where we slept, but I think it was around Tenejapa. When I woke up I was in a grove of oranges, limes, and bananas beside a big river. Later we climbed a high hill and walked through a forest. "Ay, Lord! Why did I come here?" I was missing my parents terribly and felt very sad.

The people I was with had very little food, and it was hardly fit to eat anyway. Oh, dear God! No salt! I more or less ate some beans and a little tortilla. But I didn't want to stay with them, and about three weeks later I left their little house. I walked back down the hill and put my faith in God. Then I met some people on the road.

"Where are you going?" they asked.

"I'm going to San Cristóbal."

"Why don't you eat some soup before you go?"

So they took me to a house, and there they left me. Some workers were there gathering peanuts, others cutting bananas. I was afraid of them and decided not to stay.

But where was I going to find my parents? God knows where they had gone. All I know is that I don't have a memory of them. Where was I going to go? I just knew that I had to go somewhere. But what road should I take? This way, that way, or the other? So I wandered on the trails until I found a big rock and sat down.

Soon two ladies passed by and asked, "What are you doing sitting here?"

"I'm on my way to San Cristóbal," I told them.

"Do you want to go with us?"

"Yes," I said, and I went with them even though I didn't know them. What else was I going to do?

After we had walked for a long time, it began to rain very hard. Uuuyyy! I couldn't go on any longer.

One of the women said to me, "We wanted to take you with us, but you can't keep up with us. So you're going to have to stay in that house over there and see if they will give you something to eat."

I entered the house and saw that two families were living there. Soon the mother came in and began to heat up some food. They gave me a tamale. How wonderful it tasted. I usually didn't like tamales, but I was so hungry that I ate it anyway. With hunger, you can eat just about anything. Afterwards, someone brought me a goatskin to lie on.

"Where are you going?" they asked.

"I'm going to San Cristóbal."

"But how are you going? Why don't you just stay here?"

So I stayed with them for about a month. But before long, a group of men passed by, looking for food. I was afraid of them and started running. I ran and ran until I came to another ranch.

The maid came out and asked, "What are you doing?"

"I'm going to San Cristóbal," I said.

"And where is your mother?" she asked.

"I don't have a mother. I don't have a father. I don't have a-n-y-b-o-d-y!"

"Who did you come with, then?"

"I came all a-l-o-o-o-n-e."

She took me into the house and asked me, "Are you hungry?"

"Yes, I'm very hungry."

She gave me a little bit of beans, a piece of cheese, and a cup of coffee and told me, "Now you're going to stay here with us."

But while I was eating, a mean lady I had met before on the road came and stuck her head in the door.

"What are you doing here?" she barked.

"Nothing," I replied.

"You have to come with me," she said.

"Where?" I asked with suspicion.

"To my house," she answered.

"No. You're going to take me away, and then you're going to kill me."

Who was going to protect me? Oh, dear God! But the owner of the house said, "Let's go, let's go." Thank heavens for those wonderful people. They hid me at the edge of the river where no one would find me. Later they came to look for me, and the lady said, "Those people came looking for you, and they even came with armed men. But you are safe with us. Ay, dear Lord, you're still just a baby. You poor child!"

So she caressed me, bathed me, and cut my hair. Then she made me new clothes. And I stayed with them forever.

What I've done in my life is work, young lady. We ground corn on a metate and made tortillas by hand. It was so much fun. Nobody ever slept very much. We didn't go to bed until ten or eleven at night. At three o'clock in the morning I was already up, and by four I was making tortillas. What a joy!

We woke up happy, enchanted with life. After we finished making tortillas, we bathed in the river. We didn't have plumbing. Nothing. After bathing, we ate and then went back to work. You wouldn't believe how much we worked. First we cleaned the cotton, taking out the seeds and the trash. Then we rolled it into wicks and made candles to sell. In those days we didn't have candles like we have now. We decorated our candles with red, yellow, and green papers. If the candles were decorated, they sold well. If not, they would hardly sell at all.

My godmother's job was to make cigarettes. She used three kinds of paper: *orosuz*, linen, and rice paper. At night, after eating, we would bundle up the cigarettes to sell. We prepared the tobacco by sprinkling it with liquor, cloves, and lemon rind. Then we let it sit for three days. The tobacco was delicious. My dear deceased godmother made many, many cigarettes. But, you know, I never learned to smoke. What for?

But how I loved to eat! Who doesn't? I didn't like to get fat though. No. But I ate anyway. I still eat, but not as much as before. I used to love green onions. I ate lots of onions. I won't tell you I didn't. But no more. My stomach can't take it. I can eat only soft things. I used to eat everything—green tomatoes with tons of chili. I used to love chilies. But no more. They make me burp. My stomach can't stand it anymore. Now I eat a piece of chicken and some plain soup. That's all.

I grew up, got married, and had four children—two girls and two boys. One of my sons, who was a very hard worker, was killed in Soconusco de Tapachula. My other son, Alberto, lives around here and comes to visit me. My younger daughter lives in San Cristóbal with her husband. He has some ranches. My other daughter lives far away. She comes to visit when she wants to, or when she has the money. Without money, how is she going to come? And if she wants to live so far away, then she can just go! I think she just doesn't want her mother's love.

Now I live all alone in Tenejapa, but someone looks after me. I can't walk well anymore, but I'm still strong. With the blessing of God, I enjoy good health. Nowadays there's lots of sickness. People put fertilizers on their crops and cook with sugar. Aaaayyy!

How delicious the bread used to be. We ate lots of bread and corn, beans, tomatoes, potatoes, all from the holy earth. Nowadays you don't see potatoes like there used to be. Where are you going to see that now?

We used to have all kinds of sugarcane in white and red, sweet and soft. Where are you going to find cane like that now? There just isn't any. Not to mention the chicken. We used to eat lots of chicken, because we raised them at home. And they were cheap. Four chickens for twenty-five cents. So cheap! Or turkeys for fifty cents.

Everything was cheap then, but now everything is so expensive. Before, just from the pure vapor of the blessed earth came everything—potatoes, squashes, cabbage. Have you eaten a tasty chicken lately? Of course not. Now the chicken is tough, tougher than my nose!

You know what I used to eat a lot? Venison. There used to be lots of deer around here. Don Manuel Castillo had a ranch somewhere, and he brought us pieces of venison for just twenty cents.

People used to be healthier back then because there weren't any doctors. When I was growing up I never once went to a doctor. Doctors are worthless! I once knew a woman who had spots on her nose. She had problems with her liver and kidneys. They cured her with very simple medicines, herbs like "holy stick" and red cloves. They rubbed a pomade of herbs on the spots. That was her medicine. A cup of chamomile tea would make you well. A cup of mint on an empty stomach is wonderful. Now doctors just give pills and injections.

Do you know what we used for cars back then? Wagons pulled by horses or oxen. Yes, there have been many changes in Chiapas. They've destroyed the forests, for one thing. When my son bought his land, just past La Hormiga, his house was out there all by itself. A gringo lived on the corner. Oh, dear God! I prayed no one would kill him.

My *comadre*, Doña María, asked me, "Why don't you buy some land out there?"

"What do you mean? Do you want them to kill me? They're always killing people out there because there's a lot of envy," I told her.

Doña María Estrada died years ago. Her daughter lives near Na Bolom where Doña Ruby-Duby used to live, there where they used to tie up the horses when Doña Ruby-Duby went on trips to the jungle.

Ruby-Duby used to go to Tenejapa. I first met her when she was hunting rabbits out there. But now the rabbits are gone. Many things are gone. The deer too. There used to be so many things to eat. But no more. The forests were destroyed when they made the roads. The roads did away with every-thing—deer, all kinds of birds, gone.

The locusts came a long time ago. They covered the sky. And what a noise they made! They ate every leaf. Just left the sticks. Here in cold country it was-n't so bad. But in Cancuc they did away with the fruit, bananas, everything. Poor people! I used to wash clothes down at the pond. Every day the women in town swept and swept the locusts away. The government had to dig big ditches to bury them. It lasted for a long time. My children were babies when that happened, many years ago.

I lived for nine years in Cancuc. Have you been there? Oh, what a beauti-ful view! The muleteers used to pass through from Yajalón, Chilón, and Ocosingo. It was lots of fun. Great merchants from Tabasco passed through on foot. They all wore huaraches. Shoes? Of course not! Nothing but huaraches. Their sandals lasted for the round trip, there and back. How those men suffered. They carried things on their backs to sell and then brought things back. What great salesmen they were, I'll never forget. "I'll take it, wrap it up!"

But now I live in Tenejapa, and here the patron saint is San Ildefonso. Each year we make a party for Carnaval. The government gives us money for it. They send us two bulls, one for the north part of town and one for the south-ern part. One bull for each, so that we don't lose the custom.

And how I used to take walks! When I was in good shape, I used to walk all over San Cristóbal, and the next day I'd do the same in Tenejapa. I never got tired. But not anymore. I used to visit all the churches. And I used to love to visit my friends and chat. Now, when the women in Tenejapa don't have work to do, they come to sit and talk with me. I love to talk.

I can't get out like I once did. And, yes, Doña María Estrada died. My dear *comadre* María is resting now. Yes, she's finally gone. But I still haven't decided to go yet. I'm still sitting right here. Oh, my Lord!

Yes, I have had suffering in my life. But I'm still stumbling around. I don't even work anymore. And I tell you right now that I'm not afraid of anyone or anything. No, not even those from the other world.

How does that saying go? Let's see ... "Strong as an ox!"

atole: a thick, nutritious beverage made from finely ground corn mixed with water. It may be sweetened with sugar or fruit or spiced with powdered chili.

balché: a fermented drink made from the bark of the *balché* tree (*Lonchocarpus*). The bark is mixed with water and honey in a ceremonial canoe and left to ferment in the steaming jungle. Regarded as a sacred and purifying libation, *balché* is consumed in great quantities during Lacandon rituals.

chicleros: workers who tap *chicle*, the congealed sap of the tropical sapodilla tree from which chewing gum is manufactured. The chicle boom was at its height in the 1940s. By opening trails and setting up camps in the Lacandon jungle, the *chicleros* made the Maya ruins more accessible to archaeologists. To the Lacandons, they brought modern tools, new diseases, and the beginning of the end of their culture.

chicozapote: a small, round tropical fruit with a pale green skin and a sweet, slightly gritty, brownish meat.

cojolite: a large game bird related to the curassow or a varicolored cousin of the wild turkey.

comal: a flat clay or metal griddle used to cook tortillas.

Coleto: nickname for natives of San Cristóbal de las Casas, Chiapas. The term derives from the Spanish word *cola*, which means tail or, in this case, ponytail. During the colonial period, Spanish men wore their long hair tied back in a *cola*, hence the name Coleto.

compadre and *comadre*: "co-father" and "co-mother," expresses the relationship between parents and godparents. More recently the meaning has been amplified to include any close friend.

curado de tepache: a fermented fruit drink.

don and *doña*: a term of respect placed before the first name of an older man or woman, respectively.

espiritista: a female healer who cures patients by "channeling" or invoking male saints. The growing popularity of the cult presents a challenge to traditional shamans, bonesetters, midwives, and herbalists.

hach hun: literally, the "true cloth," made out of tree bark by the Lacandon Maya.

hach nok: literally, the "true tunic." The traditional dress worn by the Lacandons before store-bought cotton was available to them. The tunic was made by soaking tree bark in water and then pounding the pulp into rectangular lengths of cloth. The bark cloth was then sewn up the sides, leaving openings for the head and arms.

hach pik: the traditional "true skirt," made out of bark cloth, worn by Lacandon women.

hach u: the "true necklace," made of seeds, worn by Lacandon women.

horchata: a popular sweet Mexican drink made from boiled rice.

huipil, pl. *huipiles*: the traditional hand-woven or hand-embroidered blouse worn by Maya women. Each indigenous community has its distinctive designs and colors, easily recognizable to outsiders. Hand-crafted *huipiles* display great artistry and are a source of pride and community identity for Indian women.

"Las mañanitas": traditional Mexican song sung on birthdays or anniversaries.

lunada: an outdoor evening party planned to coincide with the full moon.

majahual: a tropical tree found in the Lacandon rainforest of Chiapas. The bark fiber is used by Lacandons to weave bags, baskets, and hammocks.

mamey: a tropical fruit with a rough brown skin, large brown seed, and a delicious, sweet, orange meat.

masa: dough made of ground corn mixed with limewater, used to make tortillas and tamales.

mayordoma (fem.) and *mayordomo* (masc.): "steward," a religious position, usually bestowed on married couples, that entails the ritual care of the saints.

nauyaca: bushmaster or fer-de-lance, a deadly poisonous snake common in the lowlands of Chiapas.

orosuz: licorice.

panela: unrefined brown sugar with a high molasses content sold in cone-shaped loafs.

posada: Christmas pageant commemorating the biblical story of Joseph and Mary's search for an inn. The term may be used to describe any type of Christmas party.

posh: a potent alcoholic beverage made from sugarcane and brewed in back-yard stills. The liquor is consumed during indigenous religious rituals, fiestas, and curing ceremonies.

pozol: a nutritious, thick gruel made of coarsely ground corn mixed with water.

tepezcuintle: a doglike rodent abundant in the tropical regions of Chiapas and the Yucatán Peninsula. It is considered a delicacy in native communities.

viuda: "widow," sometimes adopted as part of a woman's formal title, followed by the name of her deceased husband.

PEOPLE

Frans Blom (1893–1963)

The son of a prominent Danish family, Frans Blom exchanged his early philosophical pursuits for a life of adventure in the uncharted regions of Chiapas. While working as an explorer for an oil company, he came upon the ruins of ancient Maya civilization. Soon he was excavating sites in Mexico and Guatemala. After studying archaeology at Harvard University, Blom became the director of the Department of Middle American Research at Tulane University, a post he held for sixteen years. Eventually he returned to Chiapas and resumed his passion for fieldwork.

Blom's arduous expeditions resulted in the first accurate maps of the Lacandon rainforest. His numerous books and journals contain detailed descriptions of the flora and fauna of the region. Blom's vivid accounts of Palenque, Yaxchilan, and Bonampak, as well as "lost cities" still buried in the jungle, are classics in the field of archaeology.

Gertrude Duby Blom (1901–1993)

The daughter of a Protestant minister, Gertrude "Trudi" Blom grew up in Berne, Switzerland. Her early career as a photographer and reporter led to a prison sentence in Fascist Italy and to threats of internment in a Nazi detention camp at the beginning of World War II. Intrigued by the native cultures of the New World, Trudi escaped to Mexico in 1940. Continuing her career as a journalist, she wrote a series of articles on the brave peasant women who fought alongside Emiliano Zapata during the Mexican Revolution. After traveling through the remotest regions of the country, Trudi began exploring the lush jungles of Chiapas. There she met members of a small Maya tribe called the Lacandons. That dramatic encounter changed her life. Trudi's photographs soon brought the Lacandons to the attention of the world. On that first trip to the jungle, in 1943, Trudi also met her future husband, the distinguished Danish archaeologist Frans Blom.

After the couple settled in San Cristóbal de las Casas, Trudi battled, with indomitable fervor, on behalf of the Lacandon Indians and their threatened environment. In 1972 the Mexican government established 662,000 hectares as a national park in which the Lacandons were the only legal residents. The government's generous gift proved duplicitous. Without understanding the consequences, the Lacandons were urged to sign papers that permitted government-owned corporations to cut down and commercialize precious tropical hardwoods such as mahogany and cedar. The treaty, which purportedly protected the rainforest, became the instrument for its wholesale destruction. However, not all the Lacandons were so easily tricked into signing away their heritage. When asked to endorse the logging contracts, Chan K'in Viejo calmly told government officials, "I didn't plant the trees. They belong to our Lord Hächäkyum. Go ask him" (Nations 1984: 35–36).

Despite this catastrophic failure, Trudi continued her crusade to preserve the biodiversity of Chiapas. She received Sweden's prestigious Global 500 Award in 1991. In addition to books and articles on Maya culture and the vanishing rainforest, Trudi's archive of more than fifty-five thousand documentary photographs represents a monumental record of the living Maya, most notably of her friends, the Lacandons.

Trudi's reputation as a firebrand was fueled by her fierce temper. She could hurl insults in four languages. But when a handsome man caught her eye, she could play the charming coquette. Fashionably independent, Trudi loved to wear colorful ethnic clothes, bold makeup, and elaborate baubles, even on her expeditions into the jungle. Although she tended to overshadow her dashing intellectual husband, the couple remained devoted. With the rainforest still imperiled at the time of her death, Trudi's fighting spirit turned to bitter resignation. She died on December 23, 1993.

Na Bolom, the residence of Frans and Gertrude Blom in San Cristóbal de las Casas, was originally an old colonial seminary, which the couple bought and restored in 1950. Because the local Indians confused the name Blom with the Maya word *bolom*, "jaguar," Frans and Trudi decided to call their home Na Bolom, "House of the Jaguar." Upon Trudi's death, Na Bolom was declared a national monument. Surrounded by botanical gardens, the estate continues to serve as an anthropological museum, library, and cultural center. The guesthouse accommodates visiting Lacandon Indians as well as international scholars and travelers.

Robert D. Bruce (1934–1997)

An anthropologist and linguist, Robert Bruce spent most of his life studying and writing about the Lacandon Indians of Nahá. He spoke the Lacandon Maya language fluently, grew his hair long, and wore the traditional white tunic of the Lacandon men. In 1957 he began to record the myths and tales of Chan K'in Viejo, the spiritual leader of Nahá. *El libro de Chan K'in* (1974) and *Lacandon Dream Symbolism* (1975) preserve the oral traditions of the Lacandon Maya.

Bruce's friendship with the people of Nahá survived the tragic incident described by Koh María (p. 179). When Bruce died in 1997, his ashes were buried in the jungle, next to the grave of his friend, Chan K'in Viejo.

Lázaro Cárdenas (1895–1970)

Born in the state of Michoacán, Lázaro Cárdenas served as a young colonel during the Mexican Revolution, where he distinguished himself in several bloody battles against the followers of Emiliano Zapata and Francisco "Pancho" Villa. A decade later, as governor of Michoacán, he initiated his long campaign for social reform.

When Cárdenas was elected president of Mexico in 1934, he turned his attention to the redistribution of land. He broke up the large haciendas and created *ejidos*, small farms operated communally but owned by the state. Under his presidency, land reform became law. He worked tirelessly on behalf of the poor, created the national workers' union, and promoted free education. In a dramatic move, he nationalized Mexico's railroads and expropriated foreign oil companies. On the international front, Cárdenas offered asylum to Leon Trotsky and to political exiles of the Spanish Civil War.

A farsighted populist and man of the people, Cárdenas became one of the most beloved presidents in Mexican history.

Venustiano Carranza (1859–1920)

Born into a family of wealthy landowners in Coahuila, Mexico, Carranza entered the political arena at an early age, first as mayor, then as state legislator, and eventually as provisional governor of his state. At the dawn of the Mexican Revolution, he allied himself with Francisco I. Madero, and the two men plotted the overthrow of the Porfirio Díaz dictatorship. A man of giant stature and regal carriage, Carranza was, by then, fifty years old.

After Madero was murdered in 1913, Carranza led his troops against federal forces. At the Convention of Guadalupe, rebel leaders elected him First Chief of the newly formed Constitutional Army. A clash of personalities between Carranza and Pancho Villa created an irreparable split in the revolutionary movement. Emiliano Zapata sided with Villa, and they called for Carranza's resignation. But after General Álvaro Obregón defeated Villa in a resounding military victory, Carranza achieved national power in 1915.

Carranza's preconstitutional government, established in Veracruz, attempted to address Mexico's deep-seated problems: inequality between rich and poor, the need for land reform, separation between church and state, and sovereignty over natural resources. Carranza's efforts to correct centuries of wrongs proved ineffectual. When Carranza was elected president of Mexico in 1917, his enemies viewed him as a man of the past. The generals of the powerful northern armies had turned to General Obregón as their leader. Forced to leave Mexico City and return to Veracruz, Carranza was ambushed and killed, most likely by supporters of Obregón, who would become the next president of Mexico.

Chan K'in Viejo (188?–1996)

Chan K'in Viejo, whose name means "Little Sun" or "Little Prophet" in the Lacandon Maya language, was the *to'ohil*—spiritual leader—of the Lacandon community of Nahá. As the guardian of the living traditions of his people, Chan K'in Viejo was a storehouse of knowledge about the myths and rituals surrounding the ancient gods. He spoke familiarly about his gods, as if they were dear old friends. With disarming cheer and wisdom, he protected his community against decades of pressure from the outside world.

A shaman and seer, Chan K'in Viejo was an expert on dream interpretation. He was also known for his extraordinary powers of clairvoyance. When his lifelong friend Gertrude Duby Blom was dying in San Cristóbal de las Casas and there was no means of notifying him, someone was dispatched to Nahá to bring Chan K'in to Na Bolom for a final farewell. Upon entering his house in Nahá, the messenger found Chan K'in sitting expectantly in his hammock, flanked by his two wives, each holding a small travel bag, ready for the journey. Chan K'in's only words were, "What took you so long?"

Chan K'in was a gifted storyteller whose tales were often inspired by poetic vision:

> Hächäkyum, Lord of all Lords,
> made the heavens and the forests.
> In the heavens he planted the stars
> and in the forests he planted the trees.
> Their roots go hand in hand.

When a tree falls in the forests,
a star also falls from the sky.

—Bruce, *El libro de Chan K'in*

Sadly, Chan K'in's male heirs have lost interest in the old stories and the ancient gods. When Chan K'in Viejo died on December 23, 1996, at the approximate age of 109, a great part of Lacandon Maya culture passed on with him.

Trudi Blom and Chan K'in Viejo at Na Bolom, 1993

Chencho

Ausencio Cruz Guzmán, a Chol Maya who grew up near the ancient ruins of Palenque, has served as a major informant to archaeologists, anthropologists, linguists, and ethnobotanists conducting research in the tropics of northern Chiapas.

Porfirio Díaz (1830–1915)

Porfirio Díaz, a Mixtec born in the city of Oaxaca, joined the military during the presidency of another native of Oaxaca, the illustrious Benito Juárez. As Díaz's military reputation grew, so did his thirst for power. In 1871 Díaz led a coup d'etat against Juárez and installed himself as president of Mexico. Although he held regular elections, Díaz essentially destroyed all semblances of representative government. For the next twenty-seven years he ruled as an enlightened despot.

Committed to material progress for his country, Díaz avidly courted foreign investors. American and French robber barons swiftly gained control of Mexican oil, railroads, and silver mines. European art and architecture swept the capital. The extravagances of the belle époque failed to reach remote regions such as Chiapas. And despite Díaz's grand plans for industrial development, Chiapas remained an impoverished backwater.

Prosperity had its price. Resentment against foreign influence rankled the working class and undermined Mexico's growing sense of national identity. Anyone who opposed the regime was imprisoned or done away with. Freedom of the press was eliminated. Throughout the nation, peace and order were maintained by force.

Political opposition to the Porfiriato finally came from an unlikely quarter: Francisco I. Madero, a wealthy landowner from northern Mexico. Madero's book, *The Presidential Succession of 1910*, became an instant best seller and sowed the seeds of revolution. On November 20, 1910, the people of Mexico rose up against the dictator, and Don Porfirio went into exile. He died in Paris four years later.

Lacandon Maya

The "True People," or *Hach Winik*, as they call themselves, are a small group of Maya Indians living in the rainforest of Chiapas, Mexico. With their long flowing hair, simple white tunics, and self-assured gazes, the *Hach Winik* seem to have stepped out of another time, another reality.

The original Lacandons who inhabited the region in pre-Columbian times were greatly feared by neighboring tribes because of their constant raids to acquire victims for human sacrifice. When the Spanish conquerors arrived in Chiapas in 1524, they failed to subdue the Lacandons militarily. As a result, the Lacandons were able to maintain their cultural and political autonomy (Boremanse 1998: 3). The group resisted repeated assaults until 1695, when their communities finally fell to the Spanish (de Vos 1980: 124–125, 158, 221–226). The new diseases brought by the conquerors eventually exterminated the warfaring tribe.

By the late eighteenth century, various ethnic groups escaping Spanish suppression in the Yucatán Peninsula began to repopulate the area. When the first explorers entered the jungle a hundred years later, they mistakenly called these late arrivals Lacandons. Even Trudi Blom believed the settlers were descendants of the legendary Lacandon warriors. On the other hand, the anthropologist Robert Bruce insisted that the Lacandons were descendants of the priests and kings of Palenque (Perera and Bruce 1982: 12). It was not until the 1980s that the historian Jan de Vos discovered the true Yucatecan origins of the present-day Lacandons.

During the 1940s and 1950s, *chicleros* and lumbermen, as well as explorers such as Frans and Trudi Blom, slowly penetrated the Lacandon world, bringing the modest trappings of Western civilization with them—machetes, cooking utensils, salt, store-bought cotton, and guns. But for the most part, the dense rainforest protected the Lacandons from modern culture. Today, persistent proselytizing efforts by Evangelical sects have undermined Lacandon religious beliefs and customs. Rampant deforestation, cattle ranching, and agrarian settlements pose serious threats to their traditional way of life.

About 560 Lacandons live in the four communities of Metzabok, Lacanjá Chansayab, Bethel, and Nahá. Most Lacandon boys have cut their long hair, wear jeans instead of traditional tunics, and aspire to owning a car. Young girls watch Mexican soap operas on satellite TV and dream of tall, blond boyfriends who will whisk them off to live in the big city. Few practice the intensive agriculture of their fathers. Having depleted the wildlife, men no longer hunt for game. Conservation groups have placed a moratorium on killing tropical birds for their feathers. Lacandon men and women eke out a living making hand-crafted items they seldom use—god pots, bark cloth, bows and arrows—for streams of tourists visiting the nearby Maya ruins.

The majestic mahogany, cedar, and sacred ceiba trees are almost gone now, cut down by government-owned logging companies and by new inhabitants moving into the jungle. But the waters of Lake Nahá are still clear and calm, and the roar of howler monkeys can sometimes be heard in the distance. Chan K'in Viejo prophesied that when the jungle dies, his people will die with it. His prediction has almost come true.

Pedro Meza

Pedro Meza was born in the Tzeltal Maya village of Tenejapa in 1960. When he was a boy, his mother, María Meza Girón, taught him the art of weaving, traditionally a women's occupation. At the age of sixteen, he won the National Youth Prize of Mexico. He has created more than fifteen hundred drawings of Classic Maya brocaded designs. In addition to his research on ancient textiles, he is cofounder and director of the Maya weaver's society, Sna Jolobil.

Walter F. Morris Jr.

Born in Boston, Walter "Chip" Morris first came to Chiapas in 1972 and began studying Maya culture. A collector and scholar of Maya textiles, he helped organize the weaver's society, Sna Jolobil. In 1983 he received the prestigious MacArthur Fellowship Award for his innovative study of ancient and modern Maya textile symbolism. He is the author of the acclaimed book, *Living Maya* (1987).

June Nash

June Nash, Distinguished Professor of Anthropology at City College of the City University of New York, has spent thirty years conducting research in the highlands of Chiapas, most notably in the pottery-making village of Amate-nango del Valle.

General Alberto Pineda Ogarrio (1872–1966)

Alberto Pineda grew up as the privileged son of Manuel Pineda, a prosperous landowner. While Don Manuel advocated communal lands for the Indians, his son supported the interests of conservative landholders. When, in 1917, President Venustiano Carranza began to break up the large plantations and to return the land to the Indians, Pineda rose up against the government. Honest, disciplined, and brave, the young general gained the support of wealthy merchants and property owners in San Cristóbal. Many Indians admired his courage, even though he represented the factions that wished to keep the Indians subservient (Laughlin 1988: 262).

Pineda's reputation as a military strategist was well deserved. After losing a tough battle against Carranza's federal forces in Ocosingo, Pineda evacuated his troops, along with the townsfolk of Ocosingo, by secreting them through a narrow passage left unguarded by government soldiers. Holding their breaths and muffling the horses' hooves with rags, the troops moved silently through the dark night, only a few steps away from sleeping enemy officers (García de León 1981: 296).

After the victory of the revolutionary army in 1920, Pineda reoccupied San Cristóbal, refusing to recognize the government of President Adolfo de la Huerta. But in 1924, in an incident described by Teresa Domínguez Carrascosa (p. 7–8), the Pinedists were thoroughly routed by federal forces and driven out of town. Instead of pursuing the rebels, President Huerta sent a peace agent to negotiate with the general. Pineda agreed to surrender if the government met his demands: military recognition and payment for his troops. The government complied, and the revolution in Chiapas was over.

Robert L. Rands

During forty years of excavations and analyses of pottery found at the Classic Maya site of Palenque, the archaeologist Robert Rands established the major historical periods of the ancient city. A pioneer in the field, he is currently conducting ceramics studies at the Smithsonian Center for Materials Research and Education.

Samuel Ruiz

Samuel Ruiz was the Roman Catholic bishop of San Cristóbal de las Casas from 1959 to 1999. When he was first sent to Chiapas, Ruiz was a conservative. But after he witnessed the desperate living conditions of the Indians in his diocese, his politics shifted. In the late 1960s, during a conference of Latin American bishops, he was introduced to the "theology of liberation," which stressed the church's responsibilities to the poor. The experience altered Ruiz's view of his ministry.

The bishop became increasingly vocal about the needs of the poor. He also began to build what he called *la iglesia autóctona*, a church rooted in indigenous culture. The Roman Catholic Church, present in Chiapas since the sixteenth century, had never installed Indian priests or nuns. Ruiz began training and consecrating indigenous catechists and deacons, a revolutionary act in the eyes of the Vatican. In Maya communities every man who holds religious office shares his duties with his wife; a man without a mate is considered incomplete. And so Bishop Ruiz consecrated married couples as deacons. Since the church does not permit women to officiate during services, this was considered heresy, and conservatives in the Vatican tried to remove Ruiz from office. Despite decades of opposition, Ruiz consecrated some four hundred married couples as deacons, with the right to give many of the holy sacraments.

Ruiz trained thousands of Indian catechists, who traveled to remote areas bringing the word of God to the people. Don Samuel gained countless followers among the Maya, who lovingly call him *Tatic*, "Father." He also acquired many enemies among the conservative population of San Cristóbal.

In 1988 Bishop Ruiz founded the Fray Bartolomé de las Casas Center for Human Rights, which denounced human rights violations in Chiapas. Later the bishop captured world attention when he served as mediator during peace negotiations between the Mexican government and the Zapatista Army of National Liberation, which took up arms against the government on January 1, 1994. After a brief period of violence, the Mexican government initiated talks with the rebels that ended, years later, in a controversial peace treaty.

Ruiz's ministry was fraught with tension. The conservative factions in San Cristóbal accused him of provoking and supporting the Zapatista rebels. The Vatican resisted his efforts to establish an indigenous church. After decades of pressure, Bishop Samuel Ruiz completed his appointed term of office and retired in 1999. During his farewell ceremony at the cathedral, he consecrated a number of deacons and their wives. Rome has called a moratorium on this practice.

Sna Jolobil

Founded in 1976, Sna Jolobil, "The House of the Weaver" in Tzotzil Maya, is a society made up of eight hundred women from twenty indigenous communities in the highlands of Chiapas. Its main objective is to preserve traditional textile designs, some of which date back to Classic Maya civilization.

Linda Schele

After visiting the ruins of Palenque, the artist Linda Schele became a linguist and dedicated her life to the decipherment of Maya hieroglyphic writing. With passionate intensity, she played a central role in cracking the Maya phonetic system during the 1970s. Her groundbreaking theories on Maya art, history, and cosmology appear in numerous academic articles and popular volumes, including, with David Freidel, *A Forest of Kings* (1990). A dynamic professor, she inspired hundreds of students at The University of Texas at Austin.

Marta Turok

The anthropologist Marta Turok has devoted her career to studying and promoting Mexican folk art. Having served in major government posts, she now heads the private artisan development organization, AMACUP.

Tzeltal and Tzotzil Maya

For more than a millennium, six Maya language groups have lived in Chiapas. Tzeltal and Tzotzil speakers constitute the majority.

Two thousand years ago their Tzeltalan ancestors occupied the coastal plains along the Gulf of Mexico. Gradually they moved into the highlands and by A.D. 400 settled in the mountains surrounding what is today the city of San Cristóbal de las Casas. In time they split into two distinct language groups, the Tzeltales and the Tzotziles, each with myriad dialects, customs, and costume traditions that vary from community to community. Isolated in their mountain strongholds, they were able to preserve Maya civilization centuries after the fall of the great Classic cities (Coe 1999: 34, 230–231). The Tzotziles, or People of the Bat, established a lasting reputation for their fierce independence. Tzotzil merchants of Zinacantán dominated the pre-Columbian salt trade and successfully warded off Aztec encroachment in the highlands (Laughlin 1988: 1). When the Spanish conquerors arrived in 1524, Chamula warriors withstood the siege of their citadel for three long days (Morris 1987: 22–23).

In the end, they were no match for the invaders. European illnesses decimated 90 percent of the native population (Coe 1999: 190). Under the cruel *encomienda* system, the surviving highland Maya became indentured servants, although they were allowed to retain their plots of land in the cold, inhospitable mountains. The Tzeltal Maya who remained in the tropics fared far worse. Spanish land barons seized the fertile lowlands, established huge plantations, and subjected the Indians to forced labor.

The first bishop of San Cristóbal, Bartolomé de las Casas, argued before the Spanish crown and the pope that Indians possessed souls and therefore were deserving of humane treatment. After the Spanish king abolished the *encomienda* system in 1724, priests became the principal agents of acculturation. Idolatry was crushed, yet the saints introduced to replace the Maya pantheon were welcomed as allies compatible with the old gods. Jesus became the Sun, the Virgin Mary the Moon, and the Earth Lord, god of rain and thunder, reigned over all the earth's treasures. The church rituals that evolved wove together medieval Catholicism with ancient Maya beliefs. Perhaps the clearest examples of syncretism are the large blue crosses that guard the caves, wells, and waterholes. Although they seem to be purely Christian, crosses appear in ancient Maya art as a symbol of the Tree of Life, the *axis mundi*, with its roots in the Underworld and branches in the heavens.

While outsiders may regard Maya religion as syncretic, the Tzeltales and Tzotziles consider themselves true Christians (Morris 1987: 158). Faithful to the creed, they have periodically claimed control over Catholic rituals. Two major political uprisings, the Tzeltal Rebellion of 1712 and the War of the Castes in 1868–1871, began as religious movements inspired by young Maya women. In the Tzeltal community of Cancuc, thirteen-year-old María de la Candelaria reported that the Virgin Mary had appeared to her, requesting that a chapel be built in her honor. When the Ladino priests refused to acknowledge her vision, native leaders established their own priesthood. Declaring themselves "soldiers of the Virgin," some thirty-two towns revolted against their Spanish oppressors. When they marched on San Cristóbal, the rebels were brutally slaughtered (Rosenbaum 1993: 22–23). One hundred fifty years later, Agustina Gomez Chechev, a young Tzotzil shepherdess from San Juan Chamula, discovered three stones that had fallen from the sky. The rumor spread that they were "talking stones," and soon a cult began, proclaiming Agustina the "mother of god." When the Chamulas established their own market, the irate merchants of San Cristóbal called in the army. Chamula rebels went on a rampage and murdered over one hundred ranchers before military forces crushed the rebellion and executed its leaders (Laughlin 1988: 2–3, 269–270). The victorious citizens of San Cristóbal nevertheless lived in perpetual fear, anticipating the next insurrection, the next nightmarish raid from the hills. Those fears materialized when the Zapatista Army of National Liberation marched into town at midnight on January 1, 1994. Tzeltales and Tzotziles are the backbone of the rebel movement.

Poverty, injustice, and lack of sufficient land continue to pose enormous problems. Numerous Evangelical sects threaten a social fabric in which daily customs and religious practices were once intertwined. Converts expelled from their ancestral lands as well as rural people seeking greater economic opportunities have found a refuge in the new "poverty zones" that have sprung up around San Cristóbal. Thousands more migrate to the United States.

Even traditionalists are braving the dangerous journey to "the other side." Tzotzil and Tzeltal men who have been tapped for high religious positions in their communities seek menial work in the United States in order to meet the financial responsibilities of their office. The massive exodus of indigenous men has led to an alarming rise of depression and suicide among Maya women left behind.

In traditional communities, cement houses have replaced mud and thatch huts, and local stores offer video games and Internet service. Inside the village churches, men and women recite prayers to the saints while shamans conduct curing ceremonies. Hundreds of candles illuminate the dark interior as the healers offer a sacrificial chicken and Coca-Cola to the four world directions. Against all odds, Tzotziles and Tzeltales still cling to their old way of life. "What has kept the Maya people culturally and even physically viable are their hold on the land[,] . . . a devotion to their community, and an all-pervading and meaningful belief system" (Coe 1999: 230).

Erasto Urbina (1900?–1969)

Erasto Urbina first came to public attention as a customs agent stationed on the border between Mexico and Guatemala. There he observed the steady flow of day laborers entering Chiapas to pick coffee along the coast. After witnessing the deplorable working conditions on the plantations, Urbina published damning accounts of the diseases, rotten food, and corporal punishment common in the migrant camps. Urbina's main targets were the recruiters, who plied prospective laborers with money and alcohol, then forced them to work to pay off their "debts." Lured by promises of wealth, thousands of Indians from the Chiapas highlands ended up in servitude. Urbina, in his new role as director of the Department of Indian Protection, tried to stop these abuses.

In 1936 Urbina organized the Union of Indigenous Workers, which counted thirty thousand Maya members in its ranks. In addition to defending the rights of workers, Urbina supported the Indians' demand for political control over their own communities. Finally he began preaching civil disobedience. Accompanied by bands of armed Indians, Urbina invaded a number of large ranches in the highlands, forcibly initiating long-overdue land reforms decreed by the Mexican Constitution. Landholders regarded these raids as the beginning of a new caste war.

Terrified of Urbina's radical alliance with the Indians, the elite of San Cristóbal called for his immediate resignation from his government post. Their wild plot to assassinate the charismatic leader failed miserably. Thousands of his Indian supporters surrounded San Cristóbal, and panic swept the city. Stopping short of open rebellion, the indigenous communities asked President Cárdenas to intercede on Urbina's behalf. Their petitions went unanswered. A few months later the conservatives gained control of San Cristóbal, the region, and even the Union of Indigenous Workers (García de León 1981: 413).

In a surprising twist, Erasto Urbina went on to serve as mayor of San Cristóbal in 1943. Long after his death, in 1969, he remains a legendary figure.

CUSTOMS

Carnaval

Held immediately before Lent, Carnaval is one of the largest, most colorful Catholic feast days celebrated in Latin America. As observed in indigenous communities of Chiapas, the festival coincides with the Uayab, the five "lost days" at the end of the Maya solar year when "the world is turned upside down." The celebrants include mythical characters like the *mash*, or monkeys, who are remnants of the previous creation. In Chamula the raucous New Year's ceremony ends with a fire walk, a symbolic act of purification and renewal.

Day of the Dead

In Mexico the celebrations of All Saints' Day and the Day of the Dead, on November 1 and 2, derive from pre-Columbian traditions. During these feast days, Mexican families remember their dead and celebrate the continuity of life. The occasion is neither sad nor morbid but rather an important social ritual that honors the cycle of life and death. The ancients believed that the souls of the dead return each year to visit living relatives. To welcome and guide the spirits home, family members clean the grave sites and decorate them with candles and marigolds. Food, cigarettes, liquor, sweets—whatever delicious vices the dead enjoyed during life—are offered at the graves. A special bread called *pan de muerto* (bread of the dead) is baked for this celebration, along with sugared skulls. Families spend the night in the cemetery, talking and feasting, while musicians stroll among the graves playing songs the deceased relatives enjoyed during their time on earth.

Dreams

In *Mayan Tales from Zinacantán: Dreams and Stories from the People of the Bat*, Robert M. Laughlin observes that while Westerners tend to separate dreams from "reality," in Zinacantán "it is the inner reality that motivates, explains and clarifies the irrational, hazardous events of our lives ... Dreams are the means to 'see in one's soul' or to 'see with one's soul'" (1988: 4).

As is evident among the Maya and non-Maya contributors to this book, dreams are more than fantasies or the subconscious working through of daily tensions. Francisca Gómez López, distraught by the loss of her son, discovers his tragic fate in a dream. For Victoria Aguilar Hernández, a midwife from Aguacatenango, "dreams can guide you and tell you what to do." Sebastiana Pérez Espinoza's vision of the Virgin Mary summoned her to become a nun.

Walter Morris reports that many Maya women dream that they will become weavers long before they begin to practice the art. Sometimes they dream of the symbols they will weave. On the centrality of dreams in Maya culture, Morris writes, "Daily rituals are not copies of older models but living traditions confirmed in dreams. The saints and Ancestors speak to their people of the wisdom of God.... The Maya world will continue until the dreams cease" (1987: 216).

Envy

In Mexican culture it is universally recognized that people are jealous of the possessions and good fortune of others. "If their anger and hatred become sufficiently strong, they may seek the aid of a shaman who is known to wield his power with malevolent effects" (Laughlin 1988: 7).

Envidia is a venal emotion with dangerous consequences. Throughout the highlands of Chiapas, people are genuinely fearful of the harm that may befall them if they provoke the envy of their neighbors. Blatant displays of wealth are frowned upon. A woman going to market will place a cloth over her purchases to hide them from prying eyes. Indian mothers cover their babies' faces lest some envious stranger cast the "evil eye." As an extra precaution before leaving home, the mother will sip a bit of cologne and then spit it out, in a protective spray, on the heads and arms of her children (Moscoso 1989: 83).

When a jealous person resorts to witchcraft, the victim and family must defend themselves by going to church to pray for protection. If the prayers fail, the result may be sickness, loss of home and possessions, or even death. But if their prayers are heard, the harm will return to the aggressor.

Evangelism

Since 1938 Evangelical missionaries have been spreading the word of God throughout Chiapas. The conversion of thousands of indigenous people to fundamentalist sects has created deep cultural rifts in numerous communities. San Juan Chamula, the largest indigenous community in the highlands, has been particularly afflicted by religious conflicts for decades.

Traditional Chamulas consume great quantities of *posh*, or cane liquor, as part of their healing ceremonies and annual round of church-related fiestas. (The production and sale of alcohol is a big business controlled by some of the most powerful families in the community.) For religious officials and average citizens alike, ritual drinking often becomes a serious vice. The numerous Evangelical sects proselytizing in Indian communities preach that in order to speak with God one must not drink alcohol. Many Chamulas convert simply to find a life free of the family problems associated with alcoholism. Others may join the Mormons, Baptists, or Jehovah's Witnesses to escape the costs of serving in the traditional religious hierarchy or to avoid the loss of social standing if overlooked.

Tensions between Catholics and Protestants sometimes deteriorate into witch-hunts. One neighbor may accuse another of being an Evangelist in order to expropriate his land. People in better economic circumstances, for example, María Patishtán Likanchitón, are often accused of being Evangelists in order to force upon them a religious position that demands huge financial outlays for ceremonies. By accepting the burden, they prove their loyalty to traditional practices while spending great sums of money in the community. The result for the officeholder is social prestige as well as years of debt.

In some Maya communities, Catholics and Evangelicals live side by side. In Chamula, converts are summarily driven from their land. It is estimated that half the population of Chamula has converted to one of the many Evangelical sects.

Lacandon Religion

In traditional Lacandon religious life, the men are the spiritual caretakers of the community. Each man builds his own god house, a simple thatched-roof structure with no walls. There he prays and makes offerings to Hächäkyum, creator of the forests, and to the ancient Maya gods of sun, moon, rain, and fire.

Inside the god house, each deity is represented by a "god pot," a small clay bowl with an anthropomorphic effigy attached to the rim. The men communicate with their gods by chanting and praying while burning incense in the bowls and pouring offerings of *balché* into the mouths of the effigies.

Women are not allowed to pray in or even enter the god houses. They participate in rituals by preparing food for the men and the gods in the nearby ceremonial kitchen, just as Hächäkyum's wife has done since the beginning of time.

For the past fifty years, the Lacandons have successfully warded off a stubborn host of foreign missionaries. But with the death of their spiritual leader, Chan K'in Viejo, in 1996, the battle has been lost. The younger generation has forsaken the old Maya deities. The daily fragrance of incense and the haunting chants offered to Hächäkyum have changed to Sunday morning shouts of "Jesus Saves!" Only one old man, Antonio, the son-in-law of Chan K'in Viejo, still converses with his gods. Evangelical temples have replaced the traditional god houses, which now stand like ghosts in the jungle, empty and abandoned.

Talking Boxes

Talking boxes, talking saints, and talking crosses have been part of Maya folk traditions since the Spanish Conquest and probably stem from pre-Columbian practices. Periodically the miraculous objects have fomented indigenous rebellions. The Chan Santa Cruz, or Small Holy Cross, is credited with inciting the nineteenth-century Caste Wars in the Yucatán Peninsula. According to Chiapas legends, the War of the Castes (1868–1871) resulted after a Chamula Indian shepherdess found three talking stones that fell from the sky. The cult sur-

Antonio in his god house, Nahá

rounding the talking stones soon grew into a nativist religious revival, which ended in massive bloodshed (Laughlin 1988: 269; Wilson 1972).

Although the Catholic Church frowns on the practice, the Maya in the highlands of Chiapas continue to revere and consult talking saints and boxes. Caretakers of a talking box either interpret its words or speak for it. Custodianship is a lifelong responsibility handed down from generation to generation. Charlatans who benefit financially from the possession of a talking box are accused of being mere ventriloquists.

Talking boxes are said to possess healing powers. Aside from praying for supernatural cures, devotees may ask the box to locate missing objects or to intervene in romantic matters. Great quantities of *posh* are consumed during these consultations.

EVENTS

Chichonal

In 1982 El Chichonal volcano erupted for twenty days, spewing millions of tons of ash and white-hot rocks on the surrounding countryside. Rivers of lava devoured several Zoque Indian communities in the northern part of the state of Chiapas. A blanket of gray ash covered the entire state, blocking out the sun for more than a month. The environmental equilibrium of the area was affected forever (García de León 1981: 438). Entire species of birds, butterflies, and moths had disappeared when the atmosphere finally cleared. The acid contained in the ash destroyed fifteen-hundred-year-old stuccos, bas-reliefs, and murals at ancient Maya ruins such as Palenque.

Mexican Revolution

The Mexican Revolution was a long series of struggles dominated by heroic, larger-than-life personalities. The initial uprising, fomented by Francisco I. Madero, a member of one of the richest families in Mexico, was aimed at overthrowing the twenty-seven-year dictatorship of President Porfirio Díaz, whose regime had brought about material progress at the cost of personal and national freedoms. Madero called for a revolution, with himself as provisional president. His "Plan de San Luis" opposed the authority of the central government, advocated a one-term presidency, the separation of church and state, and the redistribution of land.

On November 20, 1910, uprisings erupted throughout the nation. The most heated battles occurred in the state of Morelos, the home of Emiliano Zapata, and in Chihuahua, where Francisco "Pancho" Villa commanded thousands of peasants.

Emiliano Zapata, an illiterate Indian farmer, was disinterested in sweeping political change and blind to the power of the Catholic Church. Zapata's main quarrel was with the hacienda owners who had illegally usurped land that rightfully belonged to the Indian farmers who had worked it for generations.

The *ejido* system, communal ownership of land, was to become one of the most important results of the Mexican Revolution.

Zapata and his followers bore the image of the Virgin of Guadalupe, Mexico's patron saint, on their battle standards. Pancho Villa was another sort of man altogether, dark, vengeful, and violent. As general of the Army of the North, he proved a cunning military commander. Villa attracted democratic idealists who hated ambitious politicians. Zapata's supporters tended to be anarchists or Christian mystics (Krauze 1994: 319). Inevitably these disparate factions distrusted one another and failed to unite toward the common goal. In spite of their differences, the dictator Porfirio Díaz was finally ousted and sent into exile.

In free national elections held in November 1911, Madero was chosen president. Once in office, he faced political opposition from all sides. Two years later he was murdered in a military coup led by General Victoriano Huerta.

Over the next four years, chaos ensued. Troops under the leadership of Venustiano Carranza tried to restore the constitutional order broken by Huerta. But at the 1914 Convention held in Aguascalientes, Carranza, the "First Chief," feuded with Emiliano Zapata and Pancho Villa, who endorsed Eulalio Gutiérrez for president. The disgruntled Carranza established his own government in Veracruz. After a series of bloody battles, the Gutiérrez government collapsed, and in 1917 Carranza became president of Mexico.

That year coincided with a worldwide outbreak of Spanish influenza, which soon spread to Mexico and swept across the embattled nation. The epidemic, together with a deadly famine caused in great part by the conflict, killed three times more people than the actual fighting. One million Mexicans died between 1910 and 1920. (See Teresa Domínguez Carrascosa, p. 8; Luvia Amalia Burguete Sánchez, p. 76; and Natividad Elvira Pineda Gómez, p. 125 for descriptions of the epidemic and famine in the highlands of Chiapas.) The country was in complete turmoil, and rebels ran rampant.

The major battles of the Mexican Revolution were fought in the northern and central regions. In the southeast, Carranza's forces maintained control. The exception was in the state of Chiapas where the indigenous population sympathized with Zapata. The Maya working on coffee plantations along the Pacific coast were virtual slaves, laboring to pay off their debts to the "company store." Their cries for land and their mounting grievances against large landowners made them perfect allies of the Zapatista cause.

Carranza remained president until 1920, but instead of achieving major reforms, he ruled with an iron hand. Finally his opponents in the north forcibly removed him from office, and following his assassination, General Álvaro Obregón took over the presidency. With Obregón in power, the Mexican Revolution, for all intents and purposes, was over. A democratic revolution aimed at overthrowing a dictatorship ended by creating an equally authoritarian regime.

The result was a one-party system of government: the Institutional Revolutionary Party (PRI), ruled by an all-powerful president elected for one six-year term without the chance of reelection but with the right to choose his successor. The tradition of the *dedaso*—the outgoing president "pointing the finger at," or, in effect, choosing the new president—came to an end in 2000 when the landslide victory of Vicente Fox toppled the seventy-year rule of the PRI.

The rise of a new, educated middle class has yet to offset the alarming social and economic disparities in Mexico. These, along with the unresolved issue of land redistribution, gave birth to the Zapatista Uprising in Chiapas in 1994 and the renewed struggle among the Indian population for equality and justice.

Tlatelolco

On October 2, 1968, a student demonstration at the Plaza of Three Cultures in Mexico City ended in tragedy when hundreds of students protesting against the repressive regime of President Gustavo Díaz Ordaz were killed or wounded by army and police forces. The nation was shocked by the bloodbath and the cover-up that ensued.

Zapatistas

The Zapatista Movement, named after the famous revolutionary Emiliano Zapata, began as a guerilla organization demanding land, schools, medical care, and roads for Maya communities.

On January 1, 1994—the date the North American Free Trade Agreement (NAFTA) went into effect—rebels marched into San Cristóbal de las Casas and destroyed public records housed in the city hall. In other parts of the state, the Zapatistas took over large plantations. The worst fighting occurred in Ocosingo, where rebels and landowners lost their lives. The state of Chiapas soon became a militarized zone occupied by fifty thousand federal troops. Outnumbered and poorly armed, the rebels waged a successful media campaign that drew international attention to their cause. Their call for widespread democratic change became a factor leading to the overthrow of Mexico's ruling party, the PRI. Yet the peace talks between the Zapatistas and the government gained few measurable changes for the Indian population. Having laid down their arms, the Zapatistas established dozens of autonomous communities throughout the state. As an underground force, the movement continues to seek justice, dignity, and equality for indigenous peoples.

Boremanse, Didier
1998   *Hach Winik, the Lacandon Maya of Chiapas, Southern Mexico.*
        Albany: Institute for Mesoamerican Studies, State University of
        New York.

Bruce, Robert D.
1974   *El libro de Chan K'in.* Collección Científica. México, D.F.: Instituto
        Nacional de Antropología e Historia.

Coe, Michael
1999   *The Maya.* New York: Thames and Hudson.

de Vos, Jan
1980   *La paz del dios y del rey: La conquista de la Selva Lacandona 1525–1821.*
        Colección Ceiba. Tuxtla Gutiérrez: Gobierno del Estado de
        Chiapas.
1990   *No queremos ser cristianos: Historia de la resistencia de los Lacandones,*
        1525–1695, según testimonios españoles e indígenas. México, D.F.:
        Instituto Nacional Indigenista.
2001   *Una tierra para sembrar sueños: Historia reciente de la Selva*
        Lacandona, 1950–2000. México, D.F.: Fondo de Cultura
        Económica—CIESAS.

García de León, Antonio
1981   *Resistencia y utopía.* México, D.F.: Ediciones Era.

Gordillo y Ortiz, Octavio

1999   *Diccionario de la Revolución en el Estado de Chiapas*. San Cristóbal de las Casas: UNAM Programa de Investigaciónes Multidisciplinárias sobre Mesoamerica y el Sureste.

Krauze, Enrique

1994   *México, Biography of Power*. New York: Harper Perennial.

Laughlin, Robert M.

1988   *Mayan Tales from Zinacantán: Dreams and Stories from the People of the Bat*. Edited by Carol Karasik. Washington, D.C.: Smithsonian Institution Press.

Morris, Walter F.

1987   *Living Maya*. New York: Harry N. Abrams.

Moscoso Pastrana, Prudencio

1960   *Pinedismo en Chiapas 1916–1920*. México, D.F.: Los Talleres de la Editorial "Cultura."

1989   *Las cabezas rodantes del mal: Brujería y nahualismo en los altos de Chiapas*. México, D.F.: Miguel Ángel Porrúa Grupo Editorial.

Nations, James D.

1984   "The Lacandones, Gertrude Blom, and the Selva Lacandona." In *Gertrude Blom: Bearing Witness*, by Gertrude Duby Blum. Chapel Hill: University of North Carolina Press.

Perera, Victor, and Robert D. Bruce

1982   *Last Lords of Palenque*. Berkeley: University of California Press.

Rosenbaum, Brenda

1993   *With Our Heads Bowed: The Dynamics of Gender in a Maya Community*. Albany: Institute for Mesoamerican Studies, State University of New York.

Wilson, Carter

1972   *A Green Tree and a Dry Tree*. New York: Macmillan.

Blom, Gertrude Duby
1984   *Gertrude Blom: Bearing Witness*. Chapel Hill: University of North
        Carolina Press.

Bruce, Robert D.
1975   *Lacandon Dream Symbolism*. Mexico City: Ediciónes
        Euroamericanas.

Collier, George A., and Elizabeth Lowery Quaratiello
1994   *Basta! Land and the Zapatista Rebellion in Chiapas*. New York:
        Client Distribution Services.

Eber, Christine, and Christine Kovic
2003   *Women of Chiapas*. New York: Routledge.

Gossen, Garry H.
1974   *Chamulas in the World of the Sun: Time and Space in a Maya Oral
        Tradition*. Cambridge, Mass.: Harvard University Press.

Greene, Graham
2002   *The Lawless Roads*. Toronto: Random House.

Guiteras-Holmes, Calixta
1961   *Perils of the Soul: The World View of a Tzotzil Indian*. Chicago: Uni-
        versity of Chicago Press.

Robertson, Merle Greene
1983   *Sculpture of Palenque*. Vol. I: *The Temple of the Inscriptions*. Princeton: Princeton University Press.
1985   *Sculpture of Palenque*. Vol. II: *The Early Buildings of the Palace and the Wall Paintings*. Princeton: Princeton University Press.
1985   *Sculpture of Palenque*. Vol. III: *The Late Buildings of the Palace*. Princeton: Princeton University Press.
1991   *Sculpture of Palenque*. Vol. IV: *The Cross Group, The North Group, The Olvidado and Other Pieces*. Princeton: Princeton University Press.

Rus, Diane
1997   *Mujeres de tierra fría: Conversaciónes con las coletas*. Tuxtla Gutiérrez: Universidad de Ciencias y Artes de Chiapas.

Schele, Linda, and David Freidel
1990   *A Forest of Kings*. New York: William Morrow.

Wilson, Carter
1974   *Crazy February*. Berkeley: University of California Press.

Gayle Walker's art reflects her deep affinity with the Lacandon Maya culture of Chiapas. Born and educated in the United States, Gayle made San Cristóbal her home until her untimely death in 2006. Her paintings and photographs have been exhibited in major galleries in Mexico, the United States, and Europe and are included in private and corporate collections all over the world.

Kiki Suárez was born in Hamburg, Germany, where she studied psychology at Hamburg University. When she settled in San Cristóbal de las Casas in 1977, she took up painting. Her imaginary landscapes and colorful scenes of everyday life are popular throughout Mexico, the United States, and Japan. Along with her career as an artist, Kiki runs a local gallery and continues to practice psychotherapy. She is the mother of three sons and a devoted grandmother.